Date Due

JAN 24	MAY 0 1 1999	
APR 2 6	DEC 1 4 2002	
MAY 1 0	MAR 1 6 2004	
MAY 2 4		
JAN 1 6		
JAN 2 6 1984		
APR 2 7 1988		
FEB 1 3 1991		
FEB 2 8 1995		
APR 1 2 2001		
DEC 0 5 2002		

Clippingdale, Richard Thomas George, 1941-
    Laurier; his life and world. Toronto,
McGraw-Hill Ryerson, 1979.
    224 p. illus.
    Bibliography: p. 219-220.

1. Laurier, Wilfrid, Sir, 1841-1919.
2. Prime ministers - Canada - Biography.
3. Canada - Politics and government -
1896-1911. I. Title.
0070823022   0570877
                         6/wi 0891045

LAURIER
His Life and World

RICHARD CLIPPINGDALE

LAURIER

His Life and World

WILFRID LAURIER

General Editor: W. Kaye Lamb

Picture Editor: Paul Russell

McGraw-Hill Ryerson Limited

Toronto Montreal New York London

LAURIER: HIS LIFE AND WORLD

Copyright © McGraw-Hill Ryerson Limited, 1979.

ISBN 0-07-082302-2

1 2 3 4 5 6 7 8 9 10 BP 8 7 6 5 4 3 2 1 0 9

Printed and bound in Canada

Canadian Cataloguing in Publication Data

Clippingdale, Richard, date
    Laurier, his life and world

(Prime Ministers of Canada)

Bibliography: p.
Includes index.
ISBN 0-07-082302-2

1. Laurier, Wilfrid, Sir, 1841-1919. 2. Prime ministers — Canada — Biography.
3. Canada — Politics and government — 1896-1911.* I. Title. II. Series.

FC551.L39C55   971.05'6'0924   C78-001635-1
F1033.L39C55

TITLE PAGE
Laurier's arms, as used on
his book plate.
Public Archives Canada,
C-4493.

Contents

TO THE MEMORY OF MY PARENTS,
WITH GRATITUDE

Preface

LAURIER HAS NOT lacked for biographers, practically all of them admirers. It was and is impossible — some authors virtually imply it would be indecent or immoral — to dislike the man. His charm, his serenity, his intellect and the ups and downs of his fortunes in relation to the ebb and flow of great issues have tinged Canadians' memories of him with romance and drama. Indeed, we are still waiting for a full-scale biography of him by some critical yet objective scholar who will take up J. W. Dafoe's prescription of 1922 that Laurier should be depicted as "a man who had affinities with Machiavelli as well as with Sir Galahad."

In keeping with the general purpose of this series, and with the interested general reader rather than the academic specialist in mind, I have endeavoured to treat what I consider the most significant aspects of the interaction of Laurier the Prime Minister with his country and his times, from 1896 to 1911. In my view, Laurier was eminently suitable for the Prime Ministership of a mid-1890s Canada; and for several years of triumph he not merely governed effectively, but also did much to shape the nation's development. Yet by 1911 he no longer was adequately in touch with the country in some of its changed forms and new complexities. Electoral defeat ensued, confirmed in 1917, leaving his vindication to historians.

8

For those whose appetites may be whetted a bibliography of further readings has been included. One word of warning may be appropriate for the uninitiated in Laurier land: Sir Wilfrid is awfully hard to resist once you get to know him at all. As that jaunty journalist Edward William Thomson said of him in 1911: "He bamboozles me most sweetly, often. I know when he does it, and he knows I know. Still I am bamboozled, which is the main thing." Without any irreverence of that sort O. D. Skelton, a friend and biographer, looked back on Laurier as "the best man I have ever known. His instinctive honour, his kindliness and forgetfulness of self, that shining out of nobility and distinction which men call magnetism, made every man who entered his presence a better man for it."

I am indebted to Mr. Chris Curtis, a graduate student at Carleton University, for valuable aid in the assembling of suggestions for illustrations. And no thanks can be adequate to my wife Linda and our three children — Michelle, Heather and Robbie — for putting up with my too numerous absences from family duties.

Richard Clippingdale
Ottawa, Ont.

OPPOSITE
Laurier in 1869, when he was practising law in Arthabaska. Two years later he would be elected to the Quebec legislature and launched on his half-century-long political career.
Public Archives Canada, C-1969.

1
Triumph and Deliverance

THE SCENE was the spanking new Massey Hall, at Shuter and
Victoria Streets in Tory Protestant Toronto. It was approaching eight in the evening on Friday, June 12, 1896. In 11 days
the seventh general election for the Dominion of Canada would
take place. Street cars were still disgorging hordes of citizens,
but only to swell the thousands who milled angrily about the
closed doors of the Hall, long since jammed to overflowing.
Now and then, some young men tried fruitlessly to scale the
windows in order to force entry. A hastily arranged overflow
meeting in a nearby auditorium absorbed only a small portion
of the crowd. Inside Massey Hall, as eight o'clock arrived, the
guest of honour was escorted to the stage by the mayor and
the Premier of the province. For several minutes he stood
beaming and waving to the excited audience as the applause
thundered around him.

Wilfrid Laurier, the 54-year-old French-Canadian Roman
Catholic leader of the federal Liberals, was on the very verge
of power, and he knew it. Victory was in the air this night
deep in the heartland of the Conservatives, where solid support
for Sir John A. Macdonald had given him smashing triumphs
in the previous four general elections. But now Macdonald
was five years in his grave and the political wheel of fortune
was about to turn. This tall, slim, elegant French Canadian
with the aristocratic features and the greying hair sweeping
back from around his high forehead was superbly equipped
for the challenge of power in the mid-1890s. And the Canadians, at last, were ready to give him the opportunity. Many —

Zoë Lafontaine about the time of her marriage to Wilfrid Laurier in 1868. *Public Archives Canada, C-15558.*

not only Liberals — looked eagerly to him for the conciliatory and creative leadership so desperately needed by a nation long distracted by its internal divisions and perplexed by the slow pace of its economic development. There would be fifteen brilliant busy years of his "sunny way" administration, of the "growing time," and of a vast change in Canadian life. In the beginning at least, Laurier seemed almost made to order for his and his country's opportunities.

His success was all the more striking because of his quite humble origins. He was born on November 20, 1841 in the little village of St. Lin, on the River Achigan, 25 miles north of Montreal. His father, Carolus, was a farmer and land surveyor, whose family traced its *Canadien* beginnings to a follower of Maisonneuve at the founding of Montreal in 1642. Wilfrid's parents were ambitious for their obviously intelligent son and they somehow arranged for him a good, even somewhat special, education. Three years at the local parish school were followed by two in the neighbouring community of New

Glasgow, amid Scottish schoolroom discipline and Presbyterian ways. It was an unorthodox experience for a young Catholic *Québecois*, and it put him on the road to being at ease in the other Canadian culture. An already bookish boy in his mother tongue, he began now to delight in the treasures of English poetry and prose.

At 12, he was off to the college at L'Assomption, 20 miles to the east of St. Lin. There, under priestly tutelage, he spent seven years studying French and Latin, as well as some mathematics, philosophy, history and English literature. It was the traditional background for a career at the bar, and it was followed by three years in the Faculty of Law at McGill University in Montreal. In 1864 he graduated with high marks and took up the practice of law in Montreal. Slim, over six feet tall, his boyish face topped by a shock of slightly curling chestnut hair and dominated by an aquiline nose and quick bright eyes, he was marked by many who knew him as a young man with distinctly promising prospects, slightly put into question, however, by his near impecuniousness and persistent frail health.

Politics fascinated and quickly entangled him. His family had long revered Louis-Joseph Papineau, the great *Patriote* tribune and leader of the ill-fated rebellion of 1837. For Laurier, in spite of the clerical conservatism which had surrounded him during his years at the college in L'Assomption, it was natural that the *Rouges* should be his party. They had developed in the 1840s and 1850s as a continuation of the tradition of Papineau's political radicalism and as an offshoot too of contemporary European movements of resistance to vested political, social and clerical interests. A great many of the French-Canadian *Rouges* were deeply committed as well to the survival and confirmation of their linguistically defined *nation*, French Canada. Republicanism inclined quite a few of them to support closer ties with the United States, even in some cases to the extent of favouring annexation to that country. In addition, many in the Party were deeply suspicious of assimilationist attitudes and designs on the part of English-speaking British North Americans. The *Rouges*, then, had become identified by the mid-1860s with a somewhat separatist French-Canadian *nationaliste* impulse and with sometimes continentalist leanings. As the Confederation project was being spawned at the Charlottetown and Quebec Conferences of 1864, *Rouge* resistance rose predictably and sincerely. Laurier, for all his moderation, his love of the English language and his McGill training, was easily swept along in the fight against the "scheme." On the other side were ranged most of George Etienne Cartier's pro-British and anti-American Conservatives (called *Bleus* in Quebec), funded by the bulk of the largely English-speaking business community and supported strenuously by almost all of the French-speaking Roman Catholic hierarchy. Fears of republicanism American style and liberal secularism on the continental European model stoked the fires of pro-Confederate enthusiasm.

Laurier slipped easily into high *Rouge* circles in Montreal. While at McGill he had apprenticed in the law office of Rodolphe Laflamme, a prominent and very aggressive *Rouge*; and in 1865 he became the partner of another, Méderic Lanctot. Active participation in the Montreal branch of the *Institut Canadien*, a free-thinking intellectual society in which *Rouges* were dominant, followed naturally. There his acute intelligence and striking talents in debate and discussion made a marked impression. Accordingly, when in 1866 frail health dictated a move from the Montreal city environment to a country clime, the editorship of the Party's newspaper in the Eastern Townships, *Le Défricheur*, was passed to him. Its traditions were anti-clerical and thoroughly anti-Confederation; and he followed them loyally.

Sadly, his tenure was very brief as his health remained unstable and the state of his finances became appalling. In March 1867 he abandoned the editorship for a prolonged convalescence and then a grim concentration on a law practice in the attractive little Eastern Townships court town of Arthabaska, in the county of the same name, three miles south of the booming railway centre of Victoriaville. Marriage in 1868 to the attractive and effervescent Zoë Lafontaine of Montreal, whom he had met first during his McGill days, made his Arthabaska exile far more endurable. But the clear ambition of the brilliant student, the clever and engaging debater of the *Institut Canadien*, and the energetic editor of *Le Défricheur* could not be laid aside so easily. As his health improved — it became clear he had chronic bronchitis rather than tuberculosis — his income began to mount to respectable figures

Laurier's birthplace in St. Lin, Quebec. Now a national historic site, it has been restored and furnished in the style of the 1850s. Laurier always referred to himself as Wilfrid, but he was christened Henri Charles Wilfrid Laurier. *Albert Gérin-Lajoie, Parks Canada.*

Laurier in 1874, the year
in which he was first
elected to the House of
Commons.
Public Archives Canada,
PA-25392.

and the political urges in him became once again too strong to resist. In the ranks of the Liberal Party — the old *Rouge* designation was no longer customary — he commenced his long march to power and greatness.

The truly effective Prime Ministers of Canada have spent long apprenticeships amid the troubles and trivia of politics, developing truly national perspectives and yet becoming attuned to a myriad of regional, cultural and social complexities. For Laurier, the conditioning was especially lengthy — a quarter-century. It began in 1871 with his election as a Liberal member of the Quebec legislature for his home seat of Drummond-Arthabaska. Three years later he went to the House of Commons in the Liberal landslide which followed Sir John A. Macdonald's Pacific Scandal. Another three saw him with the portfolio of Inland Revenue in Alexander Mackenzie's administration and as the leading Quebec Liberal in federal politics. Through the long years of opposition which followed that government's defeat in 1878 he was the Quebec lieutenant under both Mackenzie and, from 1880, Edward Blake. After the latter's second losing campaign, in 1887, Laurier was chosen federal Liberal chief at the age of 46. It took him nine more years and two bitterly fought elections to reach power. His long road to office abounded with great obstacles. At almost every turn his further advance must have seemed highly unlikely even to him; but intelligence, charm and a natural aptitude for political manoeuvre saw him through.

His first handicap was his youthful involvement in the *Rouges* and the *Institut Canadien*. These were hardly promising beginnings from which to emerge as a representative candidate of a resolutely Catholic Quebec for the Prime Ministership of a federated Canada, for the political power of the mostly anti-Liberal Church hierarchy was awesome. With strong episcopal support, the Conservative *Bleus* had a virtual stranglehold on both federal and provincial politics in Quebec. But Laurier was by no means an anglophobe *nationaliste*, nor had he been an uncompromisingly anti-clerical *Rouge*, at any rate not for very long. His "Frenchness" went along with his English-language training as a young boy, his law degree at McGill and his continuing love of English literature and history in making him far more adaptable to bicultural and federal politics than most of his Quebec contemporaries, Liberal or *Bleu*. And in the late 1870s it was he who took the lead for the Liberals in responding realistically and sensitively to the Roman Catholic hierarchy's hostility. His famous address on "Political Liberalism," given at Quebec City in 1877, was a masterful attempt to identify his Party with the political principles of moderate British Liberalism rather than the Papally-condemned principles of the continental European brand. His declaration of the Liberals' non-hostility to the Church, if it would cease its spiritual terrorism against them, doubtless helped to clear the way eventually to more balanced two-party politics in Quebec. However, the lessening hold of the extreme aggressive clericalist "ultramontane" (over the mountains – to Rome) school on the Church, both in Quebec and at the Vatican, probably was even more significant.

Sir Richard Cartwright, ardent free trader and vigorous partisan politician. He had left the Conservative Party when Macdonald refused to make him Minister of Finance, and Laurier also declined to appoint him to that portfolio. Nevertheless he joined the cabinet as Minister of Trade and Commerce, and was one of five members who served in it throughout Laurier's 15 years in office.
Public Archives Canada, PA-25546.

In the country at large in 1877, the Quebec speech made the 35-year-old Arthabaska lawyer a national figure. The *Canadian Monthly* of Toronto commented that he had "an amount of ability, coupled with a maturity of judgment, which marks him out as a leader of party." But there was to be no swift ascent to the heights of power.

The Liberals not only collapsed in the federal election of 1878, but returned to the frustrations and limited horizons of an opposition party for election after election. In addition, with the accession to their leadership in 1880 of the brilliant Toronto lawyer Edward Blake, then only 47, Laurier's own prospects were bound to dim. Then too, although the young Catholic *Québecois* now was known nationally, the Liberal Party was still dominated in the House of Commons by its Protestant Ontario wing. Laurier's ambition certainly seemed stilled or at least stalled in the early 1880s when John Dafoe, a young reporter in the press gallery, learned that many other M.P.'s thought Laurier's career was over. He did odd jobs for Blake in the House where there were "memories only" of his eloquence. "The tall courtly figure was a familiar sight in the Chamber and in the library — particularly in the library, where he could be found every day ensconced in some congenial alcove; but the golden voice was silent."[1] The reading, the refining of his knowledge of English and of the ways of the House — these were the activities of a man whom another reporter of the day, J. S. Willison, would remember "seemed to have settled into a way of life which he was reluctant to forsake. . . . But surely there was a great reserve of ambition in Laurier which would have gone unsatisfied if he had never commanded a party and dominated a Cabinet."[2] In the mid-1880s, however, Sir John A. Macdonald held a huge majority in Quebec and triumphantly bestrode Canadian politics, while Ontario men firmly controlled Laurier's party. Liberal strength in Quebec and thus Quebec's weight in the Liberal Parliamentary Party would have to increase dramatically if that "reserve of ambition" in Laurier were to have its outlet. Meanwhile, he either bided his time or, more likely, felt obliged to take a realistic view of the political prospects.

Ironically, his Conservative opponents in Quebec and at Ottawa helped to open the way. Quebec *Bleus* were no united band of happy warriors: for some time there had been a bitter conflict between the doctrinaire clericalist ultramontane *Castor* wing (they chose the beaver as their symbol, and hence the French word for it as their name) and Joseph-Adolphe Chapleau's more moderate, more materialistic "school of Cartier." Throughout the early 1880s this savage squabbling threatened time and again to blow the Party apart. Sometimes hungrily, sometimes warily, Laurier and the provincial Liberal leader, Honoré Mercier, waited to pick up the pieces. In November 1885, the execution of the French-speaking Métis leader, Louis Riel, following his unsuccessful rebellion in the Saskatchewan country, roused a firestorm of protest in Quebec where the Macdonald government's failure to commute the death sentence was seen widely as a surrender to the blood-lust of Protestant francophobe Ontario. Mercier's *parti national*, composed of Liberals and affronted *nationaliste* and *Castor* Conservatives, was one result, and it took power in Quebec in 1887. Federally, Laurier did his best to keep pace, and with a fire and eloquence which belied his indolent image of the recent past. His rhetoric did not match Mercier's sometimes racist rabble rousing, but he did allow his blood to rise publicly from time to time. In particular, he told a giant protest rally in Montreal, just after Riel's execution: "Had I been born on the banks of the Saskatchewan I myself would have shouldered a musket." In addition, he made to the House of Commons, in March 1886, a brilliant and moving address in support of the motion of censure against the Macdonald government for permitting the hanging. A striking fact was that the speech was in English, and was so impressive that many M.P.'s of both parties were of Edward Blake's opinion that "it was the finest parliamentary speech ever pronounced in the Parliament of Canada since Confederation."

For an awed John Dafoe, peering down from the gallery, Macdonald, Blake and all the other major figures in the House were "thrown into complete eclipse by Laurier's performance."[3] The Blake-dictated party policy of condemnation of Riel's execution was in the short term a disaster — 23 English-speaking Liberals opposed it in the House — but for Laurier and his Quebec friends, electoral prospects brightened considerably. In the federal contest of 1887 the Liberals picked up 32 of the province's 65 seats, up from 13 in 1882; and their popular vote there rose from 42 per cent to almost 49. Quebec

Edward Blake, whom Laurier succeeded as leader of the Liberal Party in 1887. Brilliant but at times exasperating, Blake was too much of an individualist to be happy or successful as a party leader.
Public Archives Canada, C-3833.

was *the* area of Liberal growth, and the result there cut Macdonald's majority in half. Nevertheless, Blake, ill, discouraged and determined to retire, turned gratefully to Laurier, and asked caucus to choose him as the new leader.

Laurier did not thrust himself forward; indeed, he was quite genuinely distressed at the turn of events. He fretted about his health, his finances, his inexperience, his French-Canadian extraction, memories in English Canada of his Riel remarks, and the understandable claims to the leadership of several prospective rivals who were senior to him and who hailed from the Party's traditional heartland of Ontario. Not a few prominent Liberals felt the force of these reservations and concerns. Louis Davies of P.E.I. thought the choice of Laurier would be "the veriest piece of political Quixotism." J. D. Edgar of Ontario believed the idea "a fearful blunder." And François Langelier of Quebec worried about Laurier's "want of physical strength." But Blake's insistence and the inability of any single Ontario claimant to draw powerful support at length won over Laurier and the caucus. For Laurier there probably was also that reserve of ambition, whatever his misgivings. At first he and others in the Party toyed with the notion that the seat was merely being kept warm for Blake, until his health was restored. Soon, however, that idea was put aside, and the new chieftain settled down to wrestle with the formidable difficulties of his position.

His first Ontario tour as leader, in the summer of 1888, did not lessen his problems. Elegant, charming and interesting he might be, but as one country Grit veteran muttered to John Dafoe: "Laurier will never make a leader; he has not enough of the devil in him."[4] It would take time to establish an emotional linkage with the rank and file Liberals outside Quebec.

With each session at Ottawa, however, he grew in confidence and forcefulness; and with each golden summer back in his beloved haven in Arthabaska, he conserved and added to his emotional and physical strength. His charming squarish red brick country home, set amidst maples and bright flowers and backed by vistas of timbered hills, was his pride and joy. There neighbours and their children, friends, followers and reporters came to visit and bask in the warmth of that tranquillity which he and his amiable devoted wife Zoë so treasured. John Willison of the Toronto *Globe* came in August

1889 and was charmed by it all. And he was impressed by Laurier's "wide range of reading, . . . the solidity of his mind, the grasp and scope of his intellect, the taste and fancy of the critic and scholar." Laurier's well stocked library shelves held much of the best literature, philosophy and history, English, French and American. In particular, he was drawn to Shakespeare, to the English historian Macaulay, and to the speeches of Abraham Lincoln and the English reformer John Bright. Clearly, it was the great causes and issues which interested this untypical politician of philosophic and romantic bent. Laurier, Willison reported, "cannot fight well except his heart be in it. His heart is not in the trivialities of parish politics. But this man would be a giant in some great national crisis."[5]

Unfortunately, the first great crisis of his leadership was more his own than the nation's. Times were bad in the Liberal bastions of rural Ontario and the Maritimes where there was strong pressure for adventurous, even radical, economic policies. There was as well, with the Riel issue by no means forgotten, a need for a French-Canadian Catholic leader to direct public attention to the supposedly safer bread and butter issues. The Liberal policy of Unrestricted Reciprocity with the United States, announced in March 1888, was the result. This bold policy, as Laurier described it, perhaps won for him a closer allegiance from among the old Alexander Mackenzie style free trade Grits, at least for a time, and it certainly gave the Party in the 1891 election its best Ontario showing in almost two decades — 49.1 per cent of the vote. But it handed the aging Sir John A. Macdonald and his failing government a "loyalty" club with which to beat the allegedly pro-Yankee Liberals. And it brought into open rebellion a disgusted and affronted Edward Blake, unconsulted about the policy, unconvinced of its fiscal responsibility or that the Americans would go along with it, and worried about its probable implications for the subversion of Canadian nationality if they did so. Then came a series of disastrous federal by-election defeats in Ontario in 1891 and 1892 and a warning to Laurier from the Liberal Premier of the province, Sir Oliver Mowat, that the Party was being tainted with annexationism. A retreat was in order, and it was signalled at the national Liberal policy convention in 1893, which replaced Unrestricted Reciprocity

OPPOSITE
Honoré Mercier.
Archives nationales du Québec. Collection Initiale.

23

with a call for "freer trade with the whole world, more particularly with Great Britain and the United States."

Concerned nationalists, champions of the British connection and protected manufacturers soon tended to be less hostile to the Liberals. "It is conceded that our platform is proof against the disloyalty cry whilst the moderate character of our trade policy fails, apparently, to create alarm in monetary circles," exulted the Toronto M.P. William Mulock to Laurier. And by 1896, even the imperialist leader Colonel George Denison believed that the Liberals were "now very careful not to squint towards the United States." With the death in 1891 of Sir John A. Macdonald, with the leadership disarray into which the governing Conservatives were plunged through most of the five years of the ensuing Parliamentary term, and with the alteration in 1893 of the Liberals' trade policy, Laurier's chances of making a successful electoral bid for substantial support in English-speaking Canada were much enhanced. Wiser now about so-called bold policies, he was far better placed to strike realistically for power as the mid-1890s arrived. His conditioning for the Prime Ministership was almost complete.

One last barrier remained: the tricky and troubling Manitoba schools question. It was the culminating crisis in a protracted series of ethnic and sectarian squabbles which had poisoned Canadian politics since Riel's execution in 1885. Minority rights for Catholic schools and the French language were under heavy attack in the West and Ontario. In part, this was a reaction to the championing of Quebec's claim to religious and *nationaliste* distinctiveness by Premier Honoré Mercier and his *parti national*. Many English Canadians firmly believed that Mercier played to essentially separatist emotions and that he was endangering the principle of separation of church and state. Additional factors included the militant Anglo-Saxon racism then so widespread in the English-speaking world and the Protestant anti-Catholic feeling so powerful throughout North America. Much of English-Canadian nationalism in these years was an amalgam of these attitudes and emotions. Men such as the Conservative M.P. for North Simcoe, D'Alton McCarthy, believed that Canadian unity in future years of mass immigration from many lands required non-denominational national schools and English as the sole official language. In 1890, the Liberal Greenway government in Mani-

toba adopted this approach. The cancellation of French as an official language stirred controversy, but not on the scale of the crisis brought on by the passage of the Public Schools Act of 1890, which terminated provincial support for Catholic schools.

Catholic leaders, in Manitoba and elsewhere, soon were begging Sir John A. Macdonald to disallow the Act. He refused, feeling that English-speaking Protestants would see this as interference with provincial rights and a sellout to Catholic pressure. With his encouragement, however, the constitutionality of the new law was tested in the courts. In July 1892, a year after Macdonald's death, the Judicial Committee of the Privy Council in London pronounced it legal because it did not, in the words of the Manitoba Act, "prejudicially affect any right or privilege with respect to denominational schools which any class of persons have by law or practice in the province at the Union." Church schools had existed in 1870, but there had been no system of public financing for them.

There remained another legal recourse for the Catholics. In Section 22 of the Manitoba Act it had been laid down that if separate school rights, whenever established, were encroached upon by the province, an appeal could be made to the federal cabinet. If such remedial action as the cabinet recommended to the province were not forthcoming, Parliament could pass remedial legislation. Similar provisions existed in

A turn-of-the-century crew removes snow from Sparks Street in Ottawa. *Public Archives Canada, PA-8376.*

the British North America Act, Section 93. Not surprisingly, the Manitoba Catholics launched an appeal.

Macdonald's Conservative successors squirmed. They feared to choose between the Catholic and Protestant viewpoints involved, especially since their Party, based as it was on Catholic Quebec and Orange Ontario, was hopelessly divided on the issue, and was wracked in these years by a staggering series of leadership struggles, in part at least a reflection of that division. In addition, their stronger men all had liabilities. Sir Charles Tupper, a father of Confederation, had an all too distinct reputation for political corruption and personal vanity. Sir Hector Langevin, long the senior Quebec minister, was embroiled in a public works scandal. His strongest French-Canadian rival, Joseph Adolphe Chapleau, was unacceptable to the clericalist *Castors* in Quebec. D'Alton McCarthy had disqualified himself with his ultra-Protestant and anti-French crusades. Perhaps the ablest Conservative of all, John S. D. Thompson of Nova Scotia, was a convert to Catholicism and at first ruled himself out because of concern over likely Protestant enmity. Consequently, Macdonald's office passed for a time to a compromise candidate, the amiable aging Senator J. J. Abbott, with Thompson as his leader in the House of Commons. When Abbott's health collapsed late in 1892, Thompson did come in after all, but with the Orange leaders Mackenzie Bowell and Clarke Wallace as the Protestant "balance" in the administration.

In Abbott's government and then his own, Thompson — now Sir John — sought refuge from the Manitoba schools dilemma yet again in the courts. They were asked if it would be constitutionally proper for the federal cabinet to hear the minority's appeal. It was mostly a matter of buying time, but there was the hope too of some constitutional sanction for subsequent federal policy. Unfortunately for the government, the Judicial Committee's decision of January 1895 gave little solace: it ruled that the Manitoba Catholics had a well-founded grievance; that they had the right to appeal to the federal cabinet; but that it was up to the cabinet to grant it or not, as a matter of public policy.

Over the next year the Conservative Party all but broke apart under the strain of what to do next. Squabbles over the leadership were part of the problem. Sir John Thompson's

A military occasion at the Citadel, Quebec, in 1896. Lord and Lady Aberdeen are seated in the middle of the group, Laurier is on the Governor General's left, and Frederick Borden, Minister of Militia and Defence, is on Lady Aberdeen's right.
Public Archives Canada, C-14136.

sudden death in December 1894 prompted a prolonged struggle, resolved only when the combatants came to fear that the Governor General, Lord Aberdeen, might call on Laurier to form an administration. The new Prime Minister, Sir Mackenzie Bowell, was a senator, and had little but his seniority in the cabinet to recommend him; it was soon clear that this was not enough. Joseph Pope, who had been Macdonald's secretary, would describe the Bowell ministry as "without unity or cohesion of any kind, a prey to internal dissensions until they became a spectacle to the world, to angels and to men."[6]

It was true that the government authorized a stern remedial order to Manitoba requiring restoration of provincial support for separate schools. This followed intense pressure from Quebec's Catholic hierarchy, which held by now a virtual whip hand over the Conservative Party in the province. Nevertheless, Manitoba's utter rejection of the order did not prompt the sponsoring of remedial legislation in Parliament for almost a year, until January, 1896. By that time, the Toronto *Mail and Empire*, the chief Conservative Party paper in Ontario, was openly opposing coercion of Manitoba; and Clarke Wallace had left the government to stand with close to a score of Conservative M.P.'s prepared to vote against a remedial bill. In

July 1895 the three French-Canadian cabinet ministers resigned, doubting Bowell's sincerity about helping the Manitoba Catholics. Two later returned — for, as one wag put it, "the loaves and fishes" — but opinion in Quebec veered dangerously to the view that the government was the captive of Protestant pressure. The crowning blow to the regime's prestige came with the resignations of seven English-speaking ministers in January 1896 because of their non-confidence in Bowell's ability to supply decisive leadership. That crisis was only resolved by his agreement to be replaced at the end of the session by Sir Charles Tupper, who would lead in the general election which by law would have to follow shortly. Tupper entered the House of Commons in a by-election and tried to push a remedial Bill through before the unavoidable dissolution in April. But time was now too short — the Bill was blocked by a filibuster. At last, the voters' time arrived — and with it Wilfrid Laurier's.

Even before the schools issue developed, Laurier had feared that the ethnic and sectarian tensions of these years were full of danger for the Liberal Party. "It is manifest that we must more and more disintegrate," he warned Edward Blake in 1888. "The only redeeming feature — I am selfish enough to use the term redeeming feature — is that the other side are already more disintegrated than we are." This was small comfort for a French-speaking Catholic leader, especially when the Manitoba legislation, under the aegis of a *Liberal* government, was mooted; nor did it remove the chill from the cold warning of Sir Richard Cartwright, Laurier's Ontario lieutenant, that the Liberal M.P.'s from that province would insist on opposing disallowance action. In 1893, after the constitutionality of the Manitoba law had been upheld, William Mulock, M.P. for North York, stressed that "the feeling in Ontario is growing rapidly in favour of the complete separation of Church and State . . . the whole country is looking to you, and it would therefore be a great disappointment to the country if anything should occur to cause the people to think that you were not a safe custodian of power if the interests of the Church came into conflict with those of the State."[7] Yet there were plenty of French-speaking and/or Catholic Liberals who took an entirely opposite view. The party press in Quebec was for a long time uncompromising. As J. Israel Tarte's *Le Canadien* put it in January 1892, the

Manitoba problem was not merely a religious squabble but "a national question." Unless it could be resolved with justice for the French-speaking Catholics, *Le Canadien* added, the English-speaking Protestant majority across Canada might view the episode as an example of how to "make us English by force."

As a French Canadian, Laurier naturally sympathized with the Catholics in Manitoba. But political realism dictated extreme caution: when the issue first began to take shape he told one Quebec supporter that he would "let events unfold before making comments which for now could only have the effect of producing irritation in certain quarters." His most specific statement during the four years of litigation came in the House of Commons in 1893 when he warned that if Archbishop Taché of St. Boniface was correct in charging that Manitoba was operating Protestant rather than non-denominational schools this would be "a most infamous tyranny." But he stressed that it was up to the Conservative federal government to find out if this was true and to investigate the "facts" of the whole problem. Until then he would not commit himself on the question of federal remedial action. That same year he confided to a French-speaking journalist rather more of his thinking. Only in the event that the courts upheld the federal government's constitutional right to interfere and subsequent investigation then showed that the schools were indeed Protestant, would he "risk everything to prevent such a tyranny." Otherwise, he would be ready to give his blessing to a Manitoba school system on the New Brunswick and Nova Scotia models.[8] There the schools were all "public" and in theory non-sectarian; but in practice the grouping of Catholic students, the hiring of Catholic teachers and the provision of after-hours non-compulsory religious education could be arranged.

These themes — the public one about investigation of "the facts," and the private one about a possible compromise solution on the Maritimes model — proved central to Laurier's political strategy once the Judicial Committee's upholding of the Manitoba minority's right to appeal for remedial action was announced in January, 1895. But for some time he could not be clear whether the mounting national and party pressures on him would permit that strategy to be adopted. He

Joseph Israel Tarte.
Public Archives Canada,
PA-13027.

warned an adviser, who naively believed that Ontario's "law abiding" Protestant Liberals would now support restoration of separate school rights in Manitoba, that the tactical aspect had to be kept in view: he dared not move in advance of public opinion in Ontario. And the clear and public message from the Party's chief newspaper there, the *Globe*, was that a stance in favour of so-called "coercion" of Manitoba would be desperately unpopular. Its editor, John Willison, urged: "We ought not to forget that there is a Protestant vote in Ontario." Sir Richard Cartwright, the chief Ontario federal Liberal, warned that "a number" of the party's M.P.'s from Ontario "must oppose" any remedial intervention in Manitoba, and that there were others "whose seats will be seriously endangered if they do not." "As time goes on," warned William Mulock of Toronto, "the public mind here is settling down to the fixed view that Manitoba must be left alone." By early April, Laurier cautioned Frank Anglin, an Irish Catholic politician anxious for a pro-remedial position, that there clearly was "a deep rooted feeling" in the Protestant provinces against interference in Manitoba. He would keep silent "until I am enabled by personal intercourse with the members of my party, to ascertain how far the Protestant community can be carried."

His silence stirred concern among Catholic champions. Archbishop Langevin of St. Boniface in Manitoba warned him in May 1895 to support the Conservatives' remedial order or be seen as "our enemy. He who is not squarely for us is against us." When the aged anti-Liberal ultramontane Bishop Laflèche of Trois-Rivières openly attacked Laurier, the semi-official Liberal newspaper, *L'Electeur*, replied:

> To say to the people that Mgr. Laflèche has more confidence in the Orangiste Bowell than in the Catholic Laurier to protect our religious rights, simply makes us remember that the bishop has been enfeebled by age and invites Catholics to look for other guides than those the Church provides for them.

This would be the basis of Liberal propaganda in Quebec until victory was won the following June. Conservative incompetence and indecision on the Manitoba issue were swinging many non-Liberals in Quebec in Laurier's direction. As John Dafoe would later put it, Tarte, the Liberal organizer in the province, "was sinking test wells in Quebec public opinion with one uniform result. The issue was Laurier." In *La Semaine Réligieuse de Québec*, the editor, Abbé David Gosselin, wrote in September, 1895 that the virulent anti-Catholicism of many Ontario Tories might well require the Quebec *Bleus* to "break the alliance of 1854 to make one with other elements." By December, when the Liberals wrested two Quebec seats from the Conservatives in by-elections, the trend was clear. As Laurier put it to a friend: "the Government by their bungling and double-dealing have created an impression of distrust, which no efforts on their part have been able to dispel."[9]

Even the introduction of the long-awaited remedial Bill

in January of the new year did not do it. Laurier now nerved himself to stand up openly to the clerical pressures: he moved the "six months' hoist" of the Bill, which would mean a delay in considering it past the end of the existing Parliament. What proved to be a successful filibuster followed. It was a brilliant strategy, probably the only Parliamentary one which would have kept Protestant "provincial rights" Liberals and Quebec Catholic Liberals together in the House. The former could oppose the Bill as improper coercion of a province; the latter could denounce it as an ineffectual remedy for the aggrieved Manitoba Catholics, since adequate financing of the separate schools was not provided for in the event of provincial hostility or non-co-operation. The simple fact was that if the Liberal party was to be a *national* party, a governing instrument, it could not come out for or against separate schools as such. Laurier would need to achieve power before he could move Canadians away from polarization on the Manitoba issue, but the readiness of his party, craving popularity and office after years of divorce from both, to let him lead it down the road of conciliation and compromise, probably signalled a developing mood for both in the country.

The election campaign began formally in April. The clerical chorus in Quebec sang loudly about Laurier's treason to Catholicism; but fewer voices joined in than in the old days of Bourget and the crusades against the *Rouges* and the *Institut Canadien*. Father Lacombe, the famous missionary to the West, had warned Laurier in January to support the remedial Bill or "the episcopacy, like one man, united with the clergy, will rise to support those who may have fallen in defending us." The Liberals made sure that the letter's contents were leaked to the public, principally to win Protestant votes in Ontario. Laurier was confident that in Quebec most Liberals would not abandon him, but told a confidant that he was "passing through a very severe ordeal." Then, five weeks before polling day, the bishops in Quebec released a collective *mandement* requiring Catholics to vote for candidates pledging to support "a law restoring to the Catholic minority of Manitoba the school rights which have been recognized by the honourable Privy Council of England." There was no specific support for the Conservatives' remedial Bill and no denunciation of any party by name. Israel Tarte described it as "not as wicked as it might have been although it is doubtless directed against us." Most Quebec bishops, whatever their personal views, were unwilling to attempt a head-on clash with the developing favourite-son support for Laurier in the province. One of the few exceptions was the militant ultramontane, Laflèche of Trois-Rivières. He denounced the Liberals' compromise policy as "the affirmation of the liberalism condemned by the Church." But only nine of Quebec's 65 federal constituencies were in dioceses governed by prelates who explicitly equated a Liberal vote in 1896 with sin.

Laurier campaigned confidently, aggressively and smoothly across Ontario and Quebec through May and June. Different points were emphasized, depending on the audience. In St. Roch, Quebec he promised: "I shall settle this question to the satisfaction of all the interested parties." The presence in his government of Sir Oliver Mowat, protector of separate school rights in Ontario, who would lead a commission to arrange a settlement, would be a guarantee of success. But then he added: "if conciliation does not succeed at all, I shall exercise that constitutional recourse furnished by the law, recourse which I shall exercise completely and entirely." In his Toronto speech at Massey Hall he told his predominantly Protestant audience that the principle of provincial rights was the basis of Confederation. He asked them to take a statesmanlike view, however, of the "old idea, not in accordance with that principle" which existed in the constitution — concerning remedial powers. He planned to "appeal to the sense of justice which was implanted in everyone by the Creator. . . . But as I myself will not be coerced by anybody, so I will not consent to force coercion upon anybody."

Election day saw the Liberals take 49 of 65 seats in Quebec, and 43 of 92 in Ontario. Across the country they won 118 ridings to 88 for the Conservatives. For Wilfrid Laurier power was achieved.

It would not be enjoyed for long, however, unless he could settle the Manitoba issue. By November, he had reached an agreement with his fellow Liberals in the Manitoba government: there would be no restoration of tax-supported separate schools; but within the one public system there could be after-hours denominational religious instruction if a local school board or a certain minimum number of parents of pupils

The Governor General and Lady Aberdeen visited the Lauriers at Arthabaska in 1897. Shown seated are (left to right) Sir Wilfrid, Lady Aberdeen, Lord Aberdeen and Lady Laurier. Lady Aberdeen wrote in her journal: "They gave us a nice simple lunch in the most perfect good taste along with themselves — we photographed & were photographed — we walked up to the Church & then to the College, Sir Wilfrid admitting that he had not walked so far for months, for he is a man who never takes exercise." *Public Archives Canada, C-3775.*

of that denomination wished. Where ten pupils in any school spoke the French language or any other language than English as their mother tongue, the teaching was to be on a bilingual basis. Catholic teachers would be hired where the proportion of Catholic pupils in a school district warranted. The Manitoba Legislature then passed amendments to its educational legislation in accord with this settlement. Clerical outrage swelled in Quebec and Manitoba far more strongly than during the election campaign. Archbishop Bégin of Quebec, hitherto a moderating influence among the hierarchy, was furious at what he termed an "unjustifiable abandonment of the best established and most sacred rights of the Catholic minority." But Laurier brought the bishops to heel by adroit diplomacy with the Vatican, culminating in the mission to Canada of Mgr. Merry del Val as Papal Delegate, beginning in March 1897. By the end of the year, on del Val's advice, the Papal Encyclical *Affari Vos* was promulgated, to the effect that though the Laurier settlement was inadequate, no better one was possible in the existing Canadian political climate, and Catholics should work sincerely and with moderation to make the best they could of the situation.

As the Laurier era began, there were other clear indications of the new Prime Minister's consummate ability at consensus non-doctrinaire politics. Already, as he neared office, he had won a measure of acceptance among the business interests — normally strong supporters of the Conservatives. Long before the election he and other Liberal leaders had decided that it would be politically impossible to eliminate the principle of protection from the tariff. As John Willison, then editor of the *Globe* and later Laurier's biographer, would recall: "Whether the country understood it or not, there was deliberate adjustment of the Party to a moderate and practical fiscal policy in many of the speeches and much of the literature of the campaign."[10] In mid-election the *Globe* printed a Laurier statement that "the intention of the Liberal Party is not and never was to establish absolute free trade in this country." Laurier, it was stressed, recognized that manufacturing required "stability and permanency" if it was to prosper. In Toronto, leading members of the financial and industrial establishment were brought together with Laurier for cozy chats. Similarly, the Montreal tycoons and entrepreneurs were approached and befriended. In both cities the announcement that *the* champion of anti-reciprocity Liberalism, Premier Sir Oliver Mowat of Ontario, would serve in a Laurier Cabinet went far to efface memories of 1891. After victory, the new alliance was solidified by the denial of the finance portfolio to Sir Richard Cartwright, the "Nestor" of Free Trade, and by the appointment of a tariff commission which took voluminous evidence from businessmen and others prior to the budget of 1897 which left National Policy protection virtually untouched. As the Conservative ex-Prime Minister Sir Mackenzie Bowell sarcastically exclaimed in the Senate, the new government's economic policies were those of the "veriest Tories in the land."

With relative tranquillity now on the Catholic-Protestant and trade fronts, the country and its exciting new leader could turn from the old divisive issues of the 1880s and early 1890s. Canada was on the move at last and was beginning to feel the wider world demanding its attention, stimulating its material growth and rousing its national ambition.

2
Neighbours and Relatives

Laurier became Prime Minister in July 1896, but took some time to complete his cabinet. This lithograph was published after the last of the original 14 members, Clifford Sifton, was appointed in November. The members were (reading clockwise): Wilfrid Laurier, R. W. Scott, L. H. Davies, A. G. Blair, Clifford Sifton, William Mulock, Israel Tarte, C. A. Geoffrion, R. R. Dobell, Sydney Fisher, F. W. Borden, W. S. Fielding, Sir Oliver Mowat, Sir Richard Cartwright.
Public Archives Canada, C-1869.

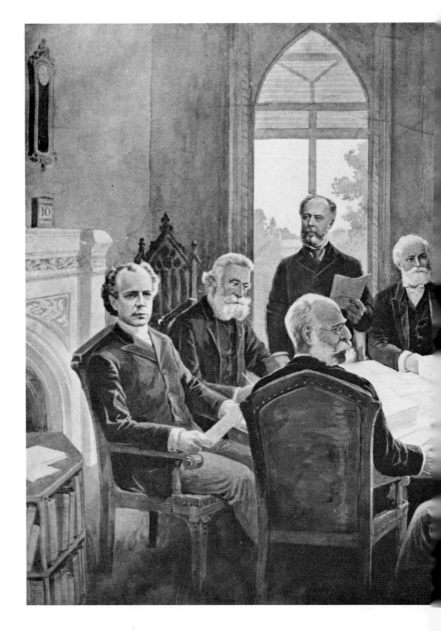

As LAURIER took office, Canadians were moving into a new era in their relations with other nations, especially with the United States and Great Britain. Over the 15 years of his Prime Ministership the power of emotions and the pull of interests made Canadians very much more involved with both those countries, and Canada's economic boom at last succeeded in claiming more British and American attention. Among Canadians, the most significant developments and changes were in attitudes.

Sir Wilfrid Laurier with a group of Canadian officers in London in 1897, at the time of Queen Victoria's Diamond Jubilee. He had just been knighted.
Public Archives Canada, C-15291.

It was nothing new for Canadians to look out on a world in which the English-speaking peoples — or "race," according to the terminology of the time — had a special position of power. However, more red colouring than ever could now be splashed on schoolroom globes to show the spectacular extent of British imperial expansion, whether in possessions or self-governing colonies, on all of the continents. It was undeniable too that the United States was an incredible success story, after it had experienced a rapid sprawling expansion across a broad continent and a stupefying surge of population and economic growth. "At the rate we are going," boasted the Toronto *Globe* in 1892, for Anglo-Saxons everywhere, "the question of what race will control the world will soon be settled."

Canadians had known for a century that their southern neighbour was powerful, wealthy, expansionist, and even dangerous, but that it was fascinating as well. Sometimes the sense of American hostility had been especially strong, as in 1812-1814, and during the Civil War and Fenian Raids crises of the 1860s; but there had been periods of closer association and mutually beneficial relations, especially during the time of the Reciprocity Treaty following 1854. Over the years there had been some significant intermingling of the two peoples. In the old Upper Canada, American settlement had made a deep imprint on political and cultural life. After Confederation hundreds of thousands of the surplus rural population of Quebec and Ontario had migrated to the mill towns of New England and to the American mid-West. American culture helped shape the lives of Canadians who stayed put, through literature, magazines and newspapers, the churches, sports and social values. English-speaking Canadians often called themselves

"British," but very many of them, whatever their origins, were increasingly North American in more ways than they may have cared to admit. And as prairie Canada opened up at century's end, hundreds of thousands from below the border joined the flood of settlement.

Still, in a Canada coming of age, national identity stemmed in large part from uneasiness about and distrust of the United States. These emotions had fed enthusiasm for Confederation in disparate colonies and later had helped push the country towards a nationalist tariff and railway policy. Lingering memories of the prosperous years under the reciprocity treaty of 1854 had died hard, but soon after 1896, when the Liberals took over in Ottawa, the extent of America's utter disdain for improved trade terms, her barring of "alien" Canadian labour and her truculence on the Alaska boundary issue, did the trick. As Governor General Lord Minto informed his brother, "constant Yankee bluff and swagger" had increased Canadians' anti-American feelings strongly. But he was sharp enough to note

The Right Honourable J. Chamberlain, Colonial Secretary.
Public Archives Canada, C-30441.

"HOME, SWEET HOME."

"Home, Sweet Home,"
a cartoon by J. W.
Bengough, originally
published September 1,
1897, shows the newly
knighted Laurier returning
home in triumph after the
trip to England for the
Diamond Jubilee and the
Colonial Conference.
Public Archives Canada,
C-8427.

the paradox that "on the other hand this insidious invasion is taking place, in speculation in minerals, lumber and large tracts of the country rented by syndicates for sport . . . [and] the tendency is to draw Canada nearer in interest and feeling to the States."[1] He might have added that the American "branch plant" industries were multiplying rapidly.

For the time being, however, the stronger pull certainly seemed to many Canadians to be towards the Britain of the "new imperialism." Traditional British lukewarmness towards the self-governing colonies was in significant measure being replaced by dreams of Empire consolidation or at least co-ordination, championed most spectacularly in politics by the dynamic Joseph Chamberlain, the Colonial Secretary. The growing competitive pressure of continental European coun-

tries and of the United States was being felt in the industrial and naval spheres in particular. This encouraged a fresh look at the colonies as allies and possible trading partners, notwithstanding the long ascendency of the dogma of free trade. Equally pragmatic concerns impelled Canadian interest. With the Americans insisting on a divided continent, commercially, Canada might have much to gain from encouraging a revitalization of the old Anglo-Canadian connection. Faster shipping and new refrigeration improvements opened a wider market for foodstuffs in the U.K.; a new flood of British immigration was available for the prairies; and London investment was needed in many spheres of production and distribution, in order to turn the developing wheat boom into a comprehensive growth.

A cartoon of Laurier by A. G. Racey of the Montreal *Star*, published late in 1897.
Public Archives Canada, C-18760.

The new economic orientation was signalled in the Laurier government's first budget, brought down in April, 1897 by W. S. Fielding. A Canadian minimum tariff (soon to be 25 per cent below the normal high protectionist one) was promised any country that would offer Canada similar or lower rates. In practice, this meant that Britain, with her free trade policy, was the chief beneficiary. One pleasing effect, at least for Canadian industrialists, was that the duties against American manufactures remained as high as ever. The Conservative-leaning civil servant Joseph Pope recorded in his diary that the government, "in bringing down a protectionist tariff, with preferential arrgt. for England, have made a big hit and completely taken the wind out of the Conservative sails."

The year of the Fielding Tariff was also the sixtieth anniversary of Queen Victoria's accession to the throne. Reflection among Canadians about the monarchy and the British connection naturally was stimulated. The Ontario romantic poet Wilfred Campbell reflected a widespread respect and affection for the monarch herself in his ode "Victoria:"

Laurier at work in his library soon after he became Prime Minister. *Public Archives Canada, C-61705.*

And we, thy loyal subjects far away
In these new lands that own thy sceptre's sway,
Betwixt thy Royal Isle and far Cathay —
Across the thunder of the western foam,
O good, grey Queen, our hearts go home, go home,
To thine and thee!
We are thine own while empires rise and wane
We are thine own for blessing or for bane,
And come the shock of thundering war again
For death or victory!

The House of Commons photographed in May 1897. Laurier is on the front bench. Parliament had met briefly in 1896, after he took office, but 1897 was his first full-scale session as Prime Minister. *Public Archives Canada, PA-12285.*

The impressive London Jubilee celebrations had their local counterparts in a thousand cities, towns and hamlets across Canada. Militia parades, patriotic speeches, dedications of monuments, band concerts, civic banquets and fireworks extravaganzas abounded. "Still Jubilating" was the Manitoba *Free Press*'s description after two weeks of it in Winnipeg. Postmaster General Mulock issued a colourful stamp of a map of the world stained with red blotches and dots and bearing the boast: "We hold a greater empire than has been." It was all very satisfying and gratifying for Canadians with their small population, vast undeveloped regions and non-identity in world

Skiing at Ottawa in 1898.
It was still a comparatively
new sport in Canada. Lord
Frederic Hamilton, ADC
to the Governor General,
introduced it in Ottawa in
1887. That year he skied
near Government House
"amidst universal
derision." Note that earlier
skiers used a single pole.
*Public Archives Canada,
PA-66618.*

affairs, to think such thoughts. They were not new of course;
but in the years of colonial development, of the achievement
of responsible government and Confederation, and of the concentration on transcontinental and industrialized national development, they had not had high priority.

A small home-grown imperialist movement had long
existed, rooted in the Loyalist heritage, in militia traditions and
in the British lifestyle, training and contacts of significant numbers of English Canada's academic and cultural upper crust.
For years the old Imperial Federation League had been the
chief institutional manifestation of that imperialism. But the
I.F.L. had not attracted much support in the 1880s — in mid-
decade there were only four branches in Canada, with a total
of about two hundred members. Not until the great debate
leading up to the 1891 election on loyalty and Unrestricted
Reciprocity did the limited appeal of theories of federalism give
way to the emotionalism which brought broader participation.
By 1891 there were 31 branches and about 1,800 members, including 760 in Toronto alone, making it the largest local chapter
in all the Empire. When divisions in the British parent federation caused dissolution of the League in the mid-1890s, the
British Empire League of Canada was formed. This organization took a less dogmatic view of the necessity of actual federation as a means to draw together the self-governing parts of
the Empire. Leaders such as Col. George T. Denison III of
Toronto, Principal George M. Grant of Queen's University
and Principal George R. Parkin of Upper Canada College were
energetic publicists of the imperial idea, and worked hard to
win general support, especially among prominent Liberals.

They correctly perceived the Party's determination, as it neared office in the mid-1890s, to wash away its old pro-American taint. Laurier's support for increased militia expenditures in the face of U.S. sabre rattling during the Venezuela Crisis of 1895-1896 and his drift towards support of a British preference tariff during his last years in opposition were appreciated. The staunch imperialism of the Liberal Premier Sir Oliver Mowat of Ontario and his chief lieutenant, George Ross, also attracted the imperialists to the Liberals, whose vigour and idealism could be contrasted favourably to the factionalism and weariness of the post-Macdonald Conservatives. Liberals were grateful for their friendship. J. S. Willison of the Toronto *Globe*, the leading English-language Liberal daily, believed that the imperialist leaders should be courted assiduously. In 1896 he went so far as to urge Laurier to make Principal Grant his chief Ontario lieutenant.

The British Empire League was hardly a mass movement, but there was no question by 1897 that a far more lively interest in the Empire and Canada's position within it was developing. The New Brunswick poet and author Charles G. D. Roberts' popular *History of Canada* came out that year, and in it he called upon Canadians to put the idea of independence behind them, as "selfish in its aims." Imperial federation, he claimed, would appeal to "a higher and broader patriotism" and it would give Canada a special mission:

> It is Canada who has taught feeble provinces how to federate, how to form a mighty commonwealth while remaining within the empire. It may be her beneficent mission, also, to lead the way toward the realization of the vaster and more glorious dream.

Lord and Lady Aberdeen in their carriage at Government House, Ottawa, in June 1898. Lord Aberdeen's term of office ended a few months later, and Lord Minto succeeded him as Governor General. Lady Aberdeen continued in her role as an important women's rights advocate of the day. In 1893 she had founded the Canadian National Council of Women.
Public Archives Canada, PA-28010.

You may talk of Billy Bryan, who grew famous by a speech,
Or tell how mighty Gladstone could the heart of England reach ;
Demosthenes you can extol--and also young McInnes ;
"Joe Howe," McGee and Thompson--though they were all "agin us."
But at utilising rhetoric, at profiting by "gab,"
This Young Tribune of the People is something of a "dab."
I made my way by talking to the Liberal leadership,
And carried the elections by an oratorical trip.

    For I am the man with the Silver Tongue.
      Also the Sunny Ways--
    I've climbed the ladder rung by rung ;
    I've found that talking pays.

But there's more in public speaking than the touching of the heart-
Of course I'm not referring to the eloquence of Tarte--
He has a way of "touching" folks in quite a different place.
He'll go and promise something while this minstrelsy I grace.
But what I meant to speak of is a habit people nourish,
Of expecting you to mean the things you utter with a flourish.
Thus when I told the farmers--"I'm a Democrat to the hilt,"
Some thought the words were golden, and sulk because they're gilt.

    This is like to tarnish the Silver Tongue
      To cloud the Sunny Ways
    What orator's heart would not be wrung
    If required to mean each phrase !

I have a patent theory which I'd put into a bill--
If I had not learned the proneness of the Senators to kill--

Requiring that all eloquence be taken on the spot ;
None may taste of it when cold--we must always
    serve it hot.
To twit a politician on a speech but two days old,
I'd punish with a dict of mutton chops grown cold.
And if a resurrectionist back of '96 should go,
I'd chain him in a graveyard near a College Medico.

    Then could I wag the Silver Tongue,
    Let shine the Sunny Ways
    Get Hansard into the furnace flung,
    And live rhetorical days.

Still it's true, I must confess it, talk pays better than you'd think ;
It's astounding what the people will gulp down without a blink.
Take those earnest Plebisciters whom I met the other day
Haven't even raised a ripple since they crossed my Sunny Way.
Should you ask me of the tariff, or the money we have spent,
I would draw myself up proudly and turn on the indig-nent.
I'm a master hand at passion, appeal and scorn and fury ;
I practise on the country what I learned before a jury ;

    For I am the Man of Majestic Pose,
      Also the Flashing Eye ;
    I've an understudy of "John A.'s" nose,
    And affect his blood-red tie.

As Laurier sailed for England to attend the Queen's Diamond Jubilee, the Toronto *Globe* remarked: "The most unimaginative must have observed that the Empire seems to be approaching the hour of some great evolutionary step in her progress."

Leaders from all over the Empire were gathering for the celebrations and to meet with the colonial secretary, Joseph Chamberlain. The London correspondent of the New York *Times* reported that

> For the first time in my experience England and the English are regarding Canadians and the Dominion with affectionate enthusiasm . . . The spirit of preference for the Mother Country appeals to the imagination here. This change will make Mr. Laurier . . . far and away the most conspicuous and popular of all the visiting premiers of the Empire.

Rudyard Kipling's poem "Our Lady of the Snows," in gratitude for the new Canadian British preference tariff, appeared in the London *Times*, ending:

> A nation spoke to a nation,
> A Queen sent word to a throne,
> Daughter am I in my mother's house,
> But mistress in my own,
> The gates are mine to open,
> As the gates are mine to close,
> And I abide by my mother's house,
> Said our Lady of the Snows.

Lord Salisbury, the British Prime Minister, wrote a Canadian friend: "I am very much gratified, as I think all concerned in public life in this country are, to observe how heartily the Dominion has accepted rallying of Liberals to the Imperial idea."

As Laurier basked in British lionization, including an unsought but politically advantageous knighthood, he used his oratorical powers spectacularly but carefully to put himself in tune with the spirit of the Jubilee emotions, in the U.K. and in Canada. In the past he had reflected privately that the British tie was gradually eroding and that the time for Canadian independence was "not I think very far away."[2] But he had long had a deep respect for British political principles and culture. Thus he could slide easily into the spirit of the "new im-

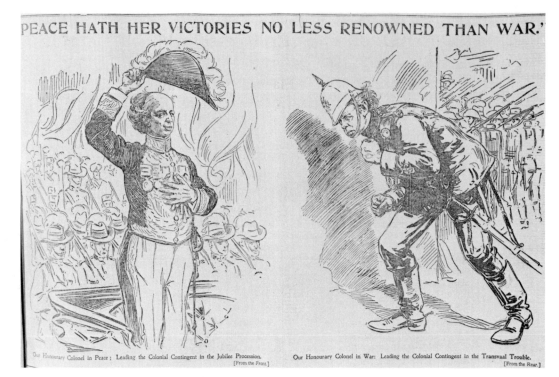

Our Honourary Colonel in Peace ; Leading the Colonial Contingent in the Jubilee Procession. [From the Front.] Our Honourary Colonel in War: Leading the Colonial Contingent in the Transvaal Trouble. [From the Rear.]

War was imminent in South Africa, and Laurier was pondering the problem of Canadian participation when this cartoon by Julien appeared in the Montreal *Star* on October 7, 1899. The Orange Free State declared war on the 12th, and the next day the Government arranged to provide a volunteer force. *Public Archives Canada, C-20442.*

OPPOSITE
Lady Laurier, a stately figure, in 1900.
Public Archives Canada, PA-27936.

perialism," but with suitable qualifications about its possible directions. His speech in Liverpool was classic. He noted that "never before" had the words "colony" and "nation" been associated together:

> All thoughts of separation disappear, thoughts of union, of a closer union, take their place. Today the sentiment exists in Canada in favour of a closer union with the motherland. The sentiment exists in Canada — nay, it exists across the ocean — from continent to continent, and today it encircles the earth. What is to be its future? It is a subject upon which I would hardly venture an opinion.

But he stressed that theorists of imperial federation had never managed to come up with a practicable scheme because "it is in the genius of British history . . . to proceed slowly, never to disturb the existing condition of things until it has become heavy, burdensome, and inadequate, amounting to a grievance, and it is to proceed only so far as may be necessary to meet existing exigencies." He thought that there now was "a colonial aspiration for a closer union, but . . . no grievance . . . The time may come when the present citizenship of the colonies . . . may become inadequate. The time may come when from the

mere aggregation of numbers . . . the sentiments and aspirations in favour of a closer union will have to be met and acknowledged and satisfied." He concluded that "the solution may be found without coming into violent conflict with the constitution of these realms, without disturbing the existing state of things on the old British principle of representation."[3]

It was all very vague, as was his rhetoric in other speeches in Britain that year. For the time being, his key words were in the resolution he pushed successfully through the Colonial Conference which followed the Jubilee — that "the present political relations between the United Kingdom and the self-governing colonies are generally satisfactory under the existing condition of things." In the military sphere he stoutly refused the pledging of Canadian assistance in British wars around the world.

The Whitely Exerciser.

The best and most popular exerciser on the market, simple and durable, can be used in any room, and is never in the way. It weighs less than 2 lbs.

A page from the 1902 Spring and Summer Eaton's catalogue. *Archives, Eaton's of Canada Limited.*

Laurier returned to Canada a conquering hero. Bonfires blazed along the St. Lawrence as his ship sailed by, and cheers and banquet tributes abounded in city after city to the special delight of Liberal organizers. Empire unity, Principal Grant wrote in the *Queen's Quarterly*, "which had so long been ridiculed . . . stood out in dramatic splendor as a real living thing, capable of being converted into an effective force." The

20.

21.

5.

6.

7.

8.

Dressmaking.

Mail order dressmaking with us has reached a high degree of excellence and satisfaction. On this page we show a few styles for the spring season, particulars of which are given below. We are always ready to execute any idea or style that customers may desire. In taking measures be exact, and always check your figures by taking a second measurement. When a perfect measurement is given a fit is guaranteed.

These prices are for making and linings only. Any ornamental trimming on the outside of the dress, such as lace, gimp, velvet, etc., must be reckoned as extras by the customer, and additional money allowed for same when ordering. To calculate the total cost of a dress, take the cost of goods and outside trimming and add our cost for making and linings.

No. 20. Girl's dress, making and linings $5 50
No. 21. Misses' dress, making and linings 6 00
No. 5. Ladies' bicycle costume, making and trimming complete, as shown in cut 10 00
No. 5. Ladies' bicycle costume, making and trimming, blazer and skirt only 8 00
No. 6. Ladies' street costume, making and linings 8 50
No. 7. Ladies' evening dress, making and linings 8 00
No. 8. Ladies' reception dress, making and linings 8 00

Where the finest superior linings are required, an extra charge of 50c. is made.

Dress material required for making 1897 styles will be as follows:

Girls' and Misses' costumes, 4½ to 5 yds ; Ladies' costumes, 6 to 6½ yds, according to size.

Ladies' costumes in 21 to 22-inch silk will require from 14 to 16 yds, and 27-inch will require 12 to 14 yds, according to size.

An extra charge is made for making silk costumes of $1.00 to 2.00, according to the style wanted.

MEASUREMENTS.

Bust (entire measurement under arm) .... Across chest ...... Around waist...... Around neck .... Width of back.... ...From neck to belt (back) .... Length of shoulder.... From neck to belt (front) .... Under arm to waist .....Inside arm (inside seam of sleeve) ...... Arm's eye ...... Around arm above elbow ...... Around hand....... Around arm below elbow ...... Around hips....... Length of skirt from belt (front)...... Length of skirt from belt (back) ....

Canadian Magazine, once truly Conservative, was unstinted in Laurier's praise:

> The man who feels that he is rising in the world is always jubilant, though naturally in a quiet way. The Canadian nation is in this position to-day, and on the crest of the rise is Sir Wilfrid Laurier. He is playing his part nobly, honourably and magnificently, and no person can grudge him what he has gained.

At the end of November came a clear sign that the Prime Minister was still on "the crest of the rise" — his candidate won a decisive by-election victory in the traditionally solid Tory seat of Centre Toronto. The conquest of Ontario as a whole awaited the next federal election.

But a real war intervened, and Laurier's "crest of the rise" was soon over, at least in Ontario. Imperialism became no more a matter of mere platform platitudes. English Canadians were caught up in the autumn of 1899 in enthusiasm for the sending of volunteers to fight for Queen and Empire in South Africa. The crisis between Britain and the two Boer Afrikaans-speaking republics was over the political rights of the English-speaking immigrants or "Uitlanders." In July the British government inquired about the possibility of a Canadian force if hostilities developed. Laurier told the Governor General that the crisis "does not seem to be one in which England, if there is war ought to ask us, or even expect us to take a part, nor do I believe that it would add to the strength of imperial sentiment to assert at this juncture, that the colonies should assume the burdens of military expenditure except . . . in the case of pressing danger." He did, however, move a resolution in the House of Commons on July 31 of sympathy for the Uitlanders in their struggle for "equal rights and liberties."

The public attitude at this point was described by an historian of the day as one of "approving indifference," since Canadians did not really expect war. By late September, however, the press was full of reports that it was imminent and that a Canadian contingent would be sent. On October 3 the *Canadian Military Gazette* printed details of plans for one, undoubtedly drawn from sources in the Militia Department. This was in spite of Laurier's firm line to the Minister of Militia, F. W. Borden, that he did not favour any such scheme. An

OPPOSITE
"Mail order dressmaking" was offered in Eaton's catalogue for the spring and summer of 1897. "We are always ready to execute any idea or style that customers may desire." Prices for the models shown varied from $5.50 to $10.00. "Where the finest superior linings are required, an extra charge of 50¢ is made." *Archives, Eaton's of Canada Limited.*

Would-be Klondikers lined up to purchase miners' licences at the Custom House at Victoria in February of 1898. *Public Archives Canada, PA-28867.*

angry Prime Minister, in a rare press interview the next day, stressed that the government had no authority from Parliament to send men overseas. Privately he raged that there was an effort "systematically planned and carried out by some military men" to force his hand. There was British pressure too: on October 3 Joseph Chamberlain cabled Lord Minto to express "appreciation" of Canadian offers to serve in South Africa.

But domestic pressure in English Canada was much more important. The Conservative mass circulation Montreal *Star* led the assault, denouncing the government's "miserable constitutional subterfuge" which was "humiliating and disgracing Canada." The *Star* arranged to have hundreds of mayors, militia commanders and other prominent Canadians telegraph their demands for action. The newspaper's headline for October 11, with Laurier still not giving in, was: "OUR COUNTRY MUST BE KEPT BRITISH: ALL CANADA RISES IN ITS MIGHT AND FORCES THE HANDS OF THE GOVERNMENT." The Ottawa *Citizen* and Toronto *Mail and Empire* adopted similar stances, as did virtually the entire Conservative English-language press. The independent Toronto *Evening News*, long rabidly anti-French Canadian, thundered that the country was "in the grip of foreigners who have no taste for British advancement. Their ideas are not those of the Anglo-Saxon. They would cast off their allegiance to Britain's queen to-morrow if they dared. Only a wholesome fear of what would happen to them at the hands of the more virile people of Ontario and the west restrains them."[4] The pressure was so strong that a loyal anti-militarist Liberal like John Cameron of the London *Advertiser* warned the Prime Minister that "we must not let this patriotic feeling be headed by the Tories. You must head it and guide it yourself." John Willison of the Toronto *Globe*, a close personal friend, told him he would either send troops or go out of office. In cabinet discussions Ontario ministers such as David Mills and William Mulock were adamant for action, the latter reportedly even storming out of one meeting when Laurier and the other Quebec members stood firm against sending troops. Especially annoying to the pro-contribution Liberals was the Minister of Public Works, J. Israel Tarte, who was adamant that there should be "not a man, not a cent for South Africa." Tarte's opposition had some anti-

Many others besides miners were attracted by the Klondike gold rush, including these ladies of doubtful repute, photographed in Dawson c.1898. *Public Archives Canada, C-18642.*

ABOVE
Yukon River steamers
compete for space at the
busy dock in Dawson
during the Klondike
gold rush.
*Public Archives Canada,
PA-13320.*

BELOW
The back-breaking climb
up the Chilkoot Pass, on
the route from Skagway
to the Klondike followed
by most of those bound
for the mines. By the

summer of 1899 a railway
had been built that gave
easy access to the interior,
but by that time the first
frantic rush was over.
*Public Archives Canada,
C-4490.*

The discoveries in the Klondike prompted searches for gold in many other places. In 1898 this miner was washing for gold in the North Saskatchewan River, just above Edmonton. *Public Archives Canada, PA-38187.*

British overtones, but Laurier, whatever his assessment of what Canada should do, sympathized strongly with the British case in South Africa which was, he told a French-Canadian correspondant, "clearly and manifestly . . . for religious liberty, political equality and civil rights."[5]

Clear principle, then, did not preclude political pragmatism. Gambling confidently that he could keep French-Canadian anti-militarist and non-imperialist isolationism under con-

A general store: they were once common but are now few and far between. The variety of goods they contrived to carry was astonishing. This one was in Dawson, where it was photographed about 1908. It was owned by Jimmy Uglow, a well-known local character and gambler, who began business by selling apples from a basket in the streets. *Public Archives Canada, C-21095.*

Bicycles enjoyed an enormous popularity in the years preceding the general availability of automobiles. Here a cycling club pauses for a rest.
Metropolitan Toronto Library Board.

trol, Laurier came up with a policy of modified participation in South Africa. The day after the Boers initiated hostilities by invading the British colonies of Cape Province and Natal, the Canadian cabinet authorized the recruitment, equipment and transportation of one thousand volunteers, to be paid and sustained in service by Britain. This decisive executive action, avoiding Parliamentary delay, was for English-Canadian opinion. The moderate expenditure, the voluntary aspect and a pledge that the contingent's despatch would be "no precedent" for future Canadian involvement in British imperial wars, were to mollify French Canadians.

Ultimately, before the Boer War concluded in 1902, Canada sent over seven thousand volunteers to South Africa. British disasters early in the struggle made the war far more than an easy "police action" and the subsequent victories, in 1900 particularly, were occasions for delirious celebrations across the country. In February, 1900 the first contingent entered major action at Paardeberg against Cronje's trapped forces. They were central to a brave charge which contributed to the Boers' surrender, thus winning the commendation of Lord Roberts, the Commander-in-Chief. Alexander Muir, author of "The Maple Leaf Forever" wrote the song "Young Canada was There" in their honour, ending:

Go, ask the hard won battle field,
Where heroes fought and fell,
Where Cronje's Boers by British pluck
Were backward hurled pell-mell,
Whose valient deeds and iron nerve
Deserve the palm to bear?

60

The answer comes with ringing cheers,
"Young Canada was there."

Chorus — Hurrah, hurrah, The Maple Leaf we'll ever
       proudly wear,
    Rallying round the Union Jack,
    Young Canada was there.

The Canadians were with Lord Roberts' spearhead when the Transvaal capital of Pretoria, the Boers' chief city, was taken in early June. A premature report on the victory reached Canada late in the evening of May 31, touching off unprecedented celebrations in the main population centres through the small hours of the morning and a workless day that followed. In Toronto, the news arrived just before midnight, and a writer of the time recorded what happened:

> Within a quarter of an hour every fire-alarm bell in the city was clanging, as if for a threatened holocaust, and one by one, as fast as the sextons could reach the ropes, the church bells took up the clamour; and wherever there was steam in powerhouses, factories and boats in the harbour, whistles screeched and roared . . . In an incredibly short time, the streets began to fill with a rapidly increasing crowd of both sexes, more or less fully dressed, hurrying toward the centre.
>
> Here wild scenes were enacted. Flags, horns and fireworks were produced, until nearly all were provided with something to wave or toot, or explode, bandsmen got instruments, pipers their pipes, impromptu processions were

Guglielmo Marconi in the Cabot Tower on Signal Hill in St. John's, Newfoundland, where in December 1901 he received the first wireless signals transmitted across the Atlantic. Six years later the first commercial wireless station capable of spanning the ocean was opened at Glace Bay, in Nova Scotia.
Newfoundland Archives.

formed, bonfires lighted even in the principal thoroughfares, and fed with anything that could be found . . . Every class was represented; the mayor proclaimed a holiday for the morrow.

The celebration did not ebb until after 3 a.m., and at dawn "the flood set in again."[6]

Anti-imperialist feeling did develop here and there in response to the South African involvement. The dashing young Liberal M.P. for Labelle, Henri Bourassa, resigned his seat on the issue, and was then triumphantly re-elected. Otherwise, the Liberal stranglehold on Quebec politics and the press held. But Bourassa had won the admiration of the increasingly numerous young *nationalistes* – students, journalists, clerics, lawyers and others. Youthful feelings boiled over in Montreal in March 1900 when French and English university students battled in the city streets for four nights. In English Canada open denunciation of the war was rare. Of the newspapers only the *Weekly Sun*, Professor Goldwin Smith's modest venture, protested, and it lost bushels of subscribers for its trouble. On the other hand, the pro-participation major dailies feasted on the public's fascination with war news. The three biggest, the Montreal *Star* and the *Globe* and *Mail and Empire* of Toronto, each picked up over ten thousand new subscribers. As Goldwin Smith lamented to a fellow anti-imperialist in England: "A tidal wave of Jingoism is now flowing."

The really serious divisions developed during the 1900 federal election campaign. Quebec rallied more strongly than ever to Laurier as a bulwark against what the Liberals successfully represented as the unrestrained military adventurism of leading English-speaking Conservatives. The government took an unprecedented 57 of Quebec's 65 seats. In the Maritimes and the West the "good times" appeals of Liberal candidates were highly successful. There would be five more Laurier supporters in Nova Scotia, four more in New Brunswick, an increase of two in Manitoba, and single additions in P.E.I. and the Territories. But Ontario stood out sharply from the general trend. Conservative propagandists there scored heavily on Laurier as "not British enough." It was charged that the government's response to the South African crisis had been dictated by a disloyal anti-British Israel Tarte. Tarte's opposition to sending a contingent was well known, and reports of

his purportedly anti-British speeches made in France while he was Canadian Commissioner to the Exposition there were given wide circulation. The chief Conservative organ in the province, the Toronto *Mail and Empire*, asked: "Is this country to remain British, is it to grow stronger and stronger under the flag; or is Mr. Tarte's hope for separation to be endorsed in this period of Imperial progress elsewhere?"[7] The *World* and *News* in the same city were even wilder in their arguments. The *World*'s summary of the election's issue was: "Are we to Be British, or Are We to Be French?"[8] The *News* called for defeat of the Liberals "who have been stirring up race feeling in Quebec as a preliminary to restoring Canada to French dominion or building up an independent French state. Canadians must decide now between Mr. Tarte's ideals and the movement to knit the Empire into one vast union."[9] It was far stronger language than that used by the Conservatives' leaders

A bride and her brides-maids in 1901, very typical of fashions and fashionable society of the time. It is difficult to imagine them taking any great interest in woman suffrage, but small groups were already active in the cause. Laurier's Franchise Act of 1898 dodged the issue by giving control of the

openly, but there was a lot of it, and the Governor General described it to his brother as "positively wicked." The result in Ontario was 55 seats for the Conservatives to 37 for the Liberals.

Almost everything Laurier had done in his first term – the British preference, maintenance of high tariffs against the U.S., the Jubilee speeches and the sending of troops to South Africa – had been with an eye to the opinion of Ontario, especially Toronto. Until the Boer War he had seemed to be on the way to solidifying his position there. Now that he had 49 of his 53-seat majority from his Quebec stronghold alone, and with Ontario the sole power base of the opposing party, Laurier had reason in the years to come to discount some Ontario opinions as guidelines for his administration's behaviour. Even in that province, with the excitement of war involvement passed, the more peaceful aspects of imperialism raised few temperatures. Canada as a whole was passing into a decade of concentration, even obsession, with domestic growth. What Laurier's major biographer would call the "flood-tide of imperialism" was beginning to ebb.

This was clearer in 1902, after the Imperial Conference following King Edward VII's coronation. Leading Canadian imperialists anticipated, as George Parkin put it, "the turning point in the history of the nation." The Canadian British Empire Leaguers called for a tax to be placed by Empire states on imports from foreign countries, with the proceeds to support imperial defence under the control of a shared council. Laurier made it perfectly clear to cabinet and Party colleagues, however, that this kind of major military commitment would be "absolutely repugnant to the convictions of all my life." He told the House of Commons that it would be suicidal to become involved in the "vortex of European militarism." As for the old chestnut of imperial preferential trade, Laurier suggested to Premier Ross of Ontario that Canadian public opinion was for protection of Canadian manufacturing, even from British competition, and that Britain was still wedded to free trade. Nevertheless, he promised the House of Commons that he would try to secure preferential treatment for the goods of Canada in the British market.

At the conference Joseph Chamberlain's efforts to get the dominions to take what he termed a "proportionate share of the

federal franchise to the provinces, which thereafter became the battleground. Finally, in 1916-1917, the five western provinces and Ontario gave women the vote. *Notman Photographic Archives, McCord Museum of McGill University.*

burdens of the Empire" got nowhere with Canada. Laurier preferred periodic conferences of first ministers to Chamberlain's proposed Council of the Empire; he stressed local militia improvement and "in due course" the establishment of local naval forces as more consonant with Canada's interest and priorities than contributions to imperial forces. On the economic front nothing really could be achieved, since Chamberlain had been unable to gain his own government's approval to breach free trade. This blunt fact would shortly push the Colonial Secretary to resign in what proved to be a protracted but futile effort to turn the British Conservative Party from free trade to imperial preference.

As for Laurier, he returned home to find general contentment with what he had done, or rather, not done. His erstwhile anti-imperialist critics in Quebec were delighted that he had stood up to the centralizers in London. Henri Bourassa would later recall that "my reconciliation with Mr. Laurier was complete."[10] A few Conservative newspapers and imperialist writers fumed, but, the B.E.L. president, Colonel Denison, told interviewers that he was "entirely satisfied" with Laurier's efforts to gain the trade preferences. Denison even conceded later that year that it would be "inadvisable for Canada to be asked to spend money on defence in any other way than under the direction of our Government, and by the hands of our own officers." But he hoped that Laurier's promises about militia improvement and local naval forces were not "merely talk." If this proved so, he wrote Chamberlain in England, he would start to put public pressure on, but "the difficulty is it would hurt Laurier in whom we base our greatest hopes of getting the French to join us in a proper scheme of Imperial defence. They have to be educated and a French Canadian alone can do it."[11] It was not merely French Canadians who required education if major moves in the imperial defence field were to be forthcoming. As John Willison, a Laurier confidant but also an imperialist, put it in a newspaper editorial in 1903: "In Canada no apprehension of a foreign war prevails. The idea of national expansion has seized upon our minds, and we are intent upon making a great nation."[12] Imperial defence, he explained to the Governor General, was "a new question for Canada." It would take time for the country to come to grips with it. Until then, he later wrote, there were only "isolated voices,"

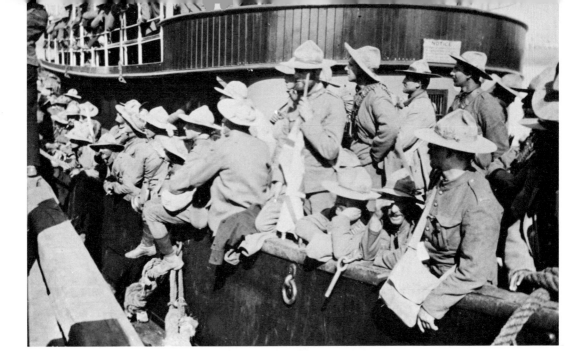

and "those who pleaded and admonished were unheard or treated merely as fretful or garrulous Imperialists."

But Canadians could become very aroused indeed over a matter of clearly *national* interests. In 1903 the Alaska boundary dispute at long last reached its climax. In 1867 the United States had purchased Alaska from Russia. Included was a thin so-called panhandle or *lisière* stretching for 600 miles down the coast beside the Yukon and British Columbia. An Anglo-Russian treaty of 1825 supposedly had settled the boundary, but precise agreement was lacking on its application. With the Canadian Yukon gold rush of the late 1890s and with the sudden influx of thousands of prospectors, a lucrative supply trade developed, and Canadian and American interests on the Pacific coast were each trying to gain the upper hand. The traditional American claim, that the panhandle included all coastal inlets, thus cutting Canada off from convenient water connection to the Yukon, was strengthened. Canada's counter-assertions were weakened by past failure to press them. The Joint High Commission of 1898-1899 almost reached a settlement: Canada was to use Pyramid Harbour on the Lynn Canal, and American sovereignty was to be retained. Unfortunately, the proposal raised a storm of criticism in the U.S. western states and was withdrawn. Subsequent efforts to refer the problem to arbitration were for some time fruitless, owing to American distrust of so-called neutral referees.

The 2nd battalion of the Canadian Mounted Rifles leaving Durban for home in 1902, at the end of the South African War. The unit had marched 2,600 miles and had taken part in 22 engagements and a number of skirmishes. *Public Archives Canada, PA-16388.*

At century's end the whole dispute was caught up in the Anglo-American diplomatic *rapprochement*. President McKinley's assassination in 1901 brought to power the impetuous, aggressive and nationalistic Theodore Roosevelt who soon proceeded with great vigour to pressure Britain to let the U.S. have its way. Canadian foreign affairs were still handled by the British Foreign Office, although in practice by this time Canada's negotiating role was considerable when her interests were directly involved. The Anglo-American arbitration treaty of January, 1903 on Alaska was not to the Laurier government's liking, yet it had little choice but to go along. The British and American sides each were to appoint three "impartial jurists of repute" to resolve the boundary issue "judicially." Canadians were horrified when President Roosevelt named his Secretary of War and two senators well known for hard-line nationalist positions on the Alaska question. The Anglo-Canadian appointees were, by contrast, in the true spirit of the treaty: Lord Alverstone, the Lord Chief Justice of England; Mr. Justice Armour of the Supreme Court of Canada; and Sir Louis Jetté, Lieutenant Governor and former member of the Superior Court of Quebec. On Armour's death, Allan Aylesworth, a leader of the Ontario bar, took over. The strength of the American case, the undeviatingly pro-United States positions of its commissioners, Roosevelt's blunt diplomatic pressures on a Britain pathetically anxious for diplomatic friendship in the face of the threat of a European power imbalance against her, and Lord Alverstone's pragmatic assessment that a final and peaceful settlement could only be substantially on American terms, produced an award to the U.S. of a wide enough panhandle to cut off all inlet access to Canadian territory and produced decisions on other aspects almost entirely in America's favour.

Canadian reaction was explosive. The two Canadian commissioners, Jetté and Aylesworth, publicly denounced the award as non-judicial and a "sacrifice of the interests of Canada." Canadians were less shocked by the Americans' behaviour than by Britain's readiness to give in to it. The Liberal Toronto *Globe* bitterly stressed that "resentment is deep and settled ... If the least backbone had been exhibited by the British Foreign Office the United States would have had to consent to real arbitration." The Liberal Manitoba *Free Press* drew some anti-imperial conclusions:

The damage is irremediable. Canadians, with very few exceptions, will accept without question the statement of their representatives that their interests were sacrificed, and the resulting resentment is certain to affect the attitude of Canada towards the United States, and in still greater degree towards the motherland.[13]

Laurier House in 1902. *Public Archives Canada, PA-8979.*

In Victoria the Conservative *Colonist* was just as blunt: "The feeling of indignation . . . is so intense that prominent citizens openly give voice to sentiments hostile to England." In Vancouver a theatre crowd booed lustily when "God Save the King" was played.

Even before the award was handed down, Laurier had cabled Clifford Sifton, the Minister of the Interior, who was acting as British Agent to the tribunal: "If we are thrown over by the Chief Justice, he will give the last blow to British diplomacy in Canada."[14] Then, when the award was debated in the House, the Prime Minister first regretted that the Americans "are very grasping in their national actions, and . . . are determined on every occasion to get the best in any agreement which they make." Then he added:

The elaborate arch (fantastic to the modern eye) erected by Canada in Whitehall, London, to celebrate the coronation of King Edward VII in 1902.
Glenbow-Alberta Institute, Calgary, Alberta.

The difficulty, as I conceive it to be, is that so long as Canada remains a dependency of the British Crown the present powers that we have are not sufficient for the maintenance of our rights. It is important that we should ask the British Parliament for more extensive powers so that if ever we have to deal with matters of similar nature again, we shall deal with them in our own way, in our own fashion, according to the best light that we have.

To take up such powers, the Governor General pointed out to him, would lead to Canada's being obliged to assume the obligations of defence, something an exceedingly non-militaristic Prime Minister was loathe to do. But more intensive Canadian involvement in British diplomacy concerning Canadian-American relations and the creation of the Department of External Affairs did follow under Laurier. However, formal constitutional change he did not press.

The anger in Canada soon subsided, aided by the reversion of the Yukon, with the gold rush over, to backwater status in terms of population and wealth. But an intensified distrust of American diplomacy remained, as did a scepticism about the coincidence of Canadian and British interests. The visiting French writer André Siegfried sized up the way things stood. He did not take seriously the Canadians' mutterings and musings about independence or what would amount to it. "They were merely having recourse," he explained in his book *The*

Race Question in Canada (1906), "by way of venting their legitimate indignation, to a method of proceeding which is always easy and sometimes effective, and which amounts in vulgar parlance to the familiar cry, 'If that's how I'm to be treated, I'm off!' " He concluded:

> After seven years of vague imperialism the Canada of 1903 we find returned to very much what we found her in 1896 — a colony essentially loyal, essentially British, but passionately. jealous of her liberties, and quite determined not to yield into any other hands whatsoever the least particle of her autonomy.

New circumstances would have to arrive if the juices of 1897-1900 were to start flowing powerfully again. Meanwhile, the new Canada was bursting at the seams with power and pride.

3
Canada's Century!

"As the nineteenth century was that of the United States, so, I think the twentieth century shall be filled by Canada." When Laurier spoke those words in 1904 few in his luncheon audience of the Ottawa Canadian Club would have thought him guilty of anything but pardonable hyperbole. The years of his Prime Ministership were a time of triumphant, unprecedented, boisterous, awe-inspiring growth in Canada.

With this expansion of enterprise, wealth and numbers, there developed among countless businessmen, politicians, professionals, journalists and writers an extraordinary sense of optimism about the Canadian future. To the Englishman J.A. Hobson, visiting the country at this time, Canada was "conscious, vocably, uproariously conscious, that her day has come . . . the poor relation has come into her fortune, a single decade has swept away all her diffidence, and has replaced it by a spirit of boundless confidence and booming enterprise."[1]

As in the days of despondency during the 1880s and early 1890s the immigration figures were probably Canadians' favourite indicators of national success or failure. Like a rising tide now, the immigrants came, from Great Britain, the United States and dozens of other lands, mostly in central and eastern Europe. In 1897, the total was only 21,716 — of which 11,383 came from Britain, 2,412 from the U.S.A. and 7,921 from "other countries." By 1901, the overall figures were more than doubled, to 55,747. Now those from other countries were most numerous, with 34 per cent, compared to 33 per cent from the U.S.A. and 22 per cent from Britain. A startling increase took place in 1903, with 138,660 coming in almost equally divided among the three sources. Two years later, British immigrants led the way once again, with 45 per cent to 30 per cent for Americans and 25 per cent for "others" — out of a total of 141,465. In 1911, the immigrants numbered an incredible 331,288, of which Britishers made up 40 per cent, Americans 30

per cent, and "others" 21 per cent. In 1913, the last full pre-war year, the total was an astonishing 400,870. Meanwhile, emigration, which previously often had exceeded immigration, plummeted. A country of 4,833,239 in 1891 had grown to 5,371,315 in 1901 and an impressive 7,203,527 in 1911.

This time of growth was often called the Wheat Boom. To be sure, the agricultural triumph of western Canada as a supplier of that staple to hungry European city dwellers was an undeniably major feature of the period. A wave of emigration out of over-populated continental Europe and Britain and a diversion of the traditional American westward migrations north to the so-called "last best West," provided the manpower

Whistle-stopping still continues, but in a greatly revised form: automobiles and airplanes have replaced the convenient platform at the back of the observation car, from which Laurier is shown speaking to a crowd of admirers at Exeter, Ontario, during the election campaign of 1904.
Public Archives Canada, C-2616.

The Governor General and Lady Minto in front of the Ice Palace in Quebec City in March 1904. *Public Archives Canada, PA-42244.*

to raise the mighty crops the markets were prepared to swallow, and at mighty prices too! New dry-farming techniques and the development of quicker-maturing wheat strains, notably Marquis, pushed the pace as well. In 1896, Canadian wheat production totalled a mere 8 million bushels. By 1901 the figure was 56 million; a decade later it was 231 million. The avalanche of numbers, in people, production and profit, pointed towards the creation of two new provinces in 1905, Alberta and Saskatchewan, and a vast enlargement of Manitoba. Where the CPR alone had serviced the transcontinental needs of the region as the old century waned, two more giant railways, the Grand Trunk Pacific and the Canadian Northern, though not fully completed in 1911, already were shouldering their shares of the heavy prairie traffic load.

One man above all others in the government and country symbolized the expansionist thrust of the Laurier years. Clifford Sifton, a rugged six-foot Manitoba lawyer, businessman and provincial cabinet minister, was sworn in as federal Minister of the Interior in 1896 at the age of 35; and he at once moved to make that previously lacklustre, red-tape-ensnarled department into the most aggressive settlement agency in Canadian history. Officials were fired or juggled; procedures for taking up homesteads were streamlined; and arrangements were made with the CPR to specify its granted acreage, thus identifying the remaining free homestead territory. Most significant of all, government officials did not just sit and wait for the world to come to western Canada; they went out to get it. Agricultural Britain was bombarded with propaganda and touring agents. Closer to home, in the United States, all stops were pulled out: newspaper advertisements abounded; there were all kinds of pamphlets on conditions in the prairies; and there were free guided tours of the developing region for American farm journalists and prospective settlers. The most difficult and controversial immigration work of these years, however, was directed at the bringing in of hundreds of thousands of continental Europeans. Some European governments actively discouraged recruitment of settlers, but Sifton managed to set up a covert Canadian operation through German steamship agents, called the North Atlantic Trading Company, to keep the flow coming steadily. Not merely the more familiar northern European immigrants were welcomed; Sifton's men also went after the ambitious among the dissatisfied peasantry elsewhere, principally from the various subject-areas of the Austro-Hungarian and Russian Empires in eastern and central Europe. "I think a stalwart peasant in a sheep-skin coat, born on the soil, whose forefathers have been farmers for ten generations, with a stout wife and a half-dozen children, is good quality," was the Minister's famous justification for introducing into Canadian society these new elements so strange to its traditional Anglo-Saxon and French complexion. There would be plenty of social consequences for all concerned, but what mattered most to immigration policy makers, in the early Laurier years at least, was that the West was being opened, and by settlers who knew how to farm and to work hard.

See Table 1 for a brief statistical survey indicating the changing ethnic make-up of the Canadian West.

Canoes are as old as Canada, but the popular use of canoes for recreation, and canoeing as a sport, are relatively recent. Here 15 members of the Carleton Place Canoe Club are enjoying an outing in 1903. The Canadian Canoe Association, which sponsors championship meets, had been organized in 1900.
Public Archives Canada, PA-58045.

TABLE 1
BIRTHPLACE OF THE PEOPLE BY PROVINCES,
1901 AND 1911[2]

	Manitoba		Saskatchewan		Alberta	
	1901	1911	1901	1911	1901	1911
Canada	180,859	264,828	55,084	248,751	41,782	162,237
British Isles	33,704	90,622	10,506	76,854	7,643	65,839
Br. Possessions	447	984	132	839	163	1,416
Br. Unknown	—	3,425	—	3,323	—	2,413
U.S.A.	6,922	16,326	2,705	69,628	11,172	81,357
Western Europe	12,095	21,633	2,820	29,829	3,652	24,828
Belgium	790	2,284	162	1,271	169	1,007
France	1,470	3,146	808	2,940	216	1,843
Germany	2,285	4,294	992	8,300	1,186	6,102
Holland	57	730	36	628	17	1,136
Iceland	5,403	5,135	271	1,337	153	235
Scandinavia	2,090	6,044	551	15,353	1,911	14,505
Eastern Europe	20,534	54,889	19,894	60,471	8,156	31,525
Austria-Hungary	11,570	37,731	7,695	35,482	5,712	21,112
Bulgaria & Romania	110	783	53	1,905	5	402
Russia	8,854	16,375	12,146	23,084	2,439	10,011
Southern Europe	128	751	6	306	78	1,922
Greece	3	64	1	40	1	97
Italy	125	687	5	266	77	1,825
China	209	844	43	1,160	234	1,784
Japan	13	19	2	58	12	244
Other	300	1,293	87	1,213	130	1,098
Total	255,211	455,614	91,279	492,432	73,022	374,663

Here then was a new region in Canada, very different from the more homogeneous populations of the older sections. More multicultural, more tied by blood to the United States than eastern Canada, freshly agrarian in an industrializing age, the West inevitably would come to see the country's problems and world situation from new perspectives. These would not always fit into the "spirit of Confederation" as conceived by the framers of the British North America Act in 1867 or by their eastern successors a half century later. It was not the first time in the nation's history that patterns of diversity and pluralism would strongly assert themselves, proving yet again that there were a multitude of Canadian realities.

OPPOSITE
A flair for the styles of the age and a face of ageless beauty and kindness, Lady Laurier in 1905.
Public Archives Canada,
C-15561.

A new population and a new dynamism did not happen only in the agricultural West. Indeed, the settlement of the prairies, crucial though it was to the boom process and mood, could not really mask the accelerating urbanization and industrialization of Canada. Between 1900 and 1910 the value of all manufactures in Canada rose from $214,526,000 to $564,467,000. Cities both in central Canada and the West mushroomed as the business of supplying the new regions and marketing their products stimulated entrepreneurial activity. Almost as many immigrants flowed into the urban East as into the countryside and towns of the West. In fact, an average of 25 to 30 per cent of the immigrants in the later Laurier years, 1905 to 1911, came to Ontario alone. Population figures for the cities in this period are instructive: see Table 2.

Chinese children on the street in Victoria in February 1900.
Provincial Archives, Victoria, B.C.

TABLE 2
POPULATION FIGURES FOR
MAJOR CANADIAN CITIES

	1891	1901	1911
Montreal	219,616	328,172	490,504
Toronto	181,215	209,892	381,833
Vancouver	13,709	29,432	120,847
Winnipeg	25,639	42,340	136,035
Hamilton	48,959	52,634	81,869
Quebec	63,090	68,840	78,710
Ottawa	44,154	59,928	87,062
Calgary	3,876	4,392	43,704
Edmonton	–	4,176	31,064
Halifax	38,437	40,832	46,619
Regina	–	2,249	30,213
Saskatoon	–	113	12,004
Saint John	39,179	40,711	42,511

Immigrants came from many countries. This trio came from Norway, the Ukraine, and England. *Public Archives Canada, PA-20915.*

Although Montreal and Toronto more than doubled their populations over the 20-year period, Winnipeg had about a 500 per cent increase and Vancouver an astonishing 800 per cent growth.

There was a dramatic and exciting acceleration of industrialization in a myriad of fields. Rubber production rose from a net value in 1900 of $606,000 to a 1910 figure of $3,438,000; boots and shoes from $7,623,000 to $16,000,000; textiles from $32,874,000 to $67,282,000; iron and its by-products from $34,967,000 to $106,313,000. There were similar patterns of growth across the board. Expectations and boasting often outdistanced even this impressive performance. When the Chambers of Commerce of the British Empire held their Congress of

Railway building and maintenance provided work and a cash income for many of the new arrivals in the West. These Slavic immigrants were working for the Ontario and Rainy River Railway, now part of the Canadian National.
Public Archives Canada, C-38826.

OPPOSITE
In this advertisement, issued in 1903, the T. Eaton Company invited incoming settlers to write for its catalogues and make use of its services. Interesting details include the bountiful harvest in the background, the CPR train (still the only one that crossed the prairies) and the labels on the suitcases, which show that the poster had American immigrants from Montana, the Dakotas and Minnesota specially in mind.
Archives, Eaton's of Canada Limited.

1903 in Montreal, that city was described to delegates as "the largest and Chief commercial city of the Dominion of Canada, a city which is at once the London, the Liverpool, the Manchester, the Birmingham, the Leeds, ... the Oxford and the Cambridge of North America." Not to be outdone, the general manager of the foundries in Sydney, Nova Scotia declared, "In the near future we will have become the manufacturing centre of the great dominion if not the whole North America." Joseph Flavelle, the Toronto pork-packer and financial manager, surveying the national wealth already developed by 1903, purred: "These drops are but the promise of the shower that is to come."

Western urban-industrial growth was particularly spectacular because it was so sudden. In the midst of the agricultural boom, urban dwellers rose from 25 per cent of the prairie population in 1901 to 35 per cent in 1911. The striking increase of the farming population of the prairies fed a huge construction industry and promoted a vast growth in numbers of grain terminals, stockyards, food processing facilities, small-scale manufacturing, wholesale businesses and financial agencies. The railway networks of three transcontinentals required an army of workers, especially in the major junction and freight marshalling facilities. In a Winnipeg rocketing to metropolitan status as the "Chicago of the North," the tattoo of the construction workers' hammers and the shadows of the so-called skyscrapers on Main Street and Portage Avenue signalled the urban boom at the gateway to the new frontier. Industrial output in Manitoba, almost wholly in Winnipeg, shot up from $13,000,000 in 1900 to $54,000,000 by 1910;

Immigrants making the transfer from ship to trains at Quebec in 1911. *Public Archives Canada, PA-10270.*

and the labour force went up from 5,000 to 17,000. Vancouver's railway and oceanic connections and the mining booms in the Klondike and the closer Kootenays pushed it ahead very fast too. Real estate prices soared. The advice on how to get rich in Vancouver was: "Take a map of the Lower Peninsula, shut your eyes, stick your finger anywhere and sit tight." Bank clearings there were the fourth highest in Canada by 1906, and a popular slogan well expressed the boisterous boosterism which characterized so many western city and business leaders:

> In nineteen-ten
> Vancouver then
> Will have one hundred thousand men
> Move her! Move her!
> Who? — Vancouver.

Edmonton saw the Canadian Northern's arrival in 1905, with the Grand Trunk Pacific not far behind. A sign of the consequences was that where there had been two wholesale houses in 1906, by 1911 there were almost 50. The Edmonton *Journal* expressed the belief that the city's future was "absolutely assured as the great metropolis of Western Canada." Calgary grew spectacularly too, on the CPR main line, and

with links to Edmonton northward and through the Crow's Nest Pass line to the Kootenays in southeastern British Columbia. The proud Calgary *Herald* pulled out all the stops in 1910: "For 150 miles to the north, south, east and west of us lies a large section of land all of which is absolutely tributary to us, rich in agriculture, in minerals, forests and natural resources, and probably without parallel in the Dominion in the possibilities of growth and development." Regina, along with Edmonton, thrived as a provincial capital city after 1905; and its metropolitan position in the most heavily populated of the prairie provinces by 1911 produced in one decade a fifteen-fold increase in population, to over 30,000, and sober expectations of a quick surge to 50,000.[3]

The processes of urbanization and industrialization characterized the economic and population growth of the Maritimes too, although at a much slower pace. Nova Scotia and New Brunswick scarcely grew at all in the 1891-1901 decade (450,396 to 459,574 and 321,263 to 331,120 respectively), but then accelerated modestly by 1911, to 492,338 for Nova Scotia and 351,889 for New Brunswick. This was quite impressive growth, given the steady decline since Confederation of profitability and employment in the former economic mainstays of the region: the export of timber, lumber products, fish and

Although conditions of entry were generous, not everyone who wanted to come to Canada was admitted. These would-be immigrants, photographed at Quebec, were being deported.
Public Archives Canada, PA-20910.

Canada West
THE LAST BEST WEST

HOMES FOR MILLIONS

RANCHING
DAIRYING
GRAIN RAISING
FRUIT RAISING
MIXED FARMING

160 ACRE FARMS IN WESTERN CANADA FREE

ISSUED BY DIRECTION OF HON. SYDNEY FISHER
MINISTER OF AGRICULTURE, OTTAWA. CANADA.

3417

wooden ships. The industrial sector had taken up the slack, even to the point that the rise of per capita industrial output in Nova Scotia exceeded that of Ontario between 1881 and 1891. Gradually, in the two decades which followed, a rather impressive array of moderate scale manufacturing flourished, notably in the textile field; and a very strong iron and steel industry prospered. Tariffs and bounties under the National Policy contributed to the growth, but central Canada's political influence prevented an alleviation of the Maritimes' competitive marketing disadvantages through an easing of freight rates on the federally owned Intercolonial Railway. And the capital accumulation resources and financing skills of Maritimers were not really competitive with the "big boys" of Montreal. First the manufacturing concerns and then, by the close of the Laurier years, the iron and steel industry, largely became tributary to, or consolidated under, these outside interests, although the process did not reach its climax in the latter area until the organization of the gigantic British Empire Steel Corporation in 1920.[4]

The Laurier years were not really boom ones in the eastern provinces, but contentment with smaller mercies can be discerned in the steady increase in support for the federal Liberals in the region. Nova Scotia's popular Premier, William Stevens Fielding, moved to the finance portfolio in Ottawa in 1896, and obliged his province faithfully with public works funds, as well as raises in appropriate tariffs and bounties protecting and stimulating local industries. Andrew Blair resigned the Premiership of New Brunswick in 1896 to take up direction of the federal railways and canals department, with similarly advantageous results. The Maritimes felt this government included them in a way no other government had since Confederation. Sir Wilfrid Laurier himself developed a strong popularity in the area, especially when he insisted in 1903 that a key feature of his mammoth Grand Trunk Pacific-National Transcontinental railway scheme should be yet another line to the Maritimes, giving the region the system's eastern terminus. Probably the best barometer of Maritime confidence and satisfaction came in the 1904 general election when the government took all 18 Nova Scotia seats, defeating even Halifax's own Robert L. Borden, the Conservative leader. To match this, New Brunswick gave 11 of its 13 seats to the

OPPOSITE
Canada West, one of hundreds of publications distributed by the federal Department of Agriculture to advertise the attractions of the Canadian West. This edition appeared in 1910. At that time the Canadian Pacific was conducting an equally energetic campaign to attract settlers. Publications appeared in many lands and in many languages.
Public Archives Canada, C-30620.

THE NEW CANADIAN BANK OF COMMERCE EDMONTON

(MATHERS 495)

A new Canadian Bank of Commerce building nearing completion in Edmonton in 1902. In the Laurier era the Bank of Commerce produced prefab branch offices of two designs in Vancouver — a simple cottage-style building, and a more modest version of this Edmonton building. These were erected in towns all over the prairies. A train of 24 cars could carry a dozen of the smaller ready-made branches.
Provincial Archives of Alberta. E. Brown Collection.

Liberals in 1908. Not until the election of 1911, when by an ironic twist the Conservatives were defending the economic status quo and the Liberals were trying to sell the virtues of change in their Reciprocity Policy, did the balance of power begin to swing back. The 1920s would see a bitter Maritime Rights attitude develop, as economic circumstances worsened. Viewed in this context, the Laurier period can be seen to have had aspects of advance and hope.

Elsewhere, there can be no doubt of the general mood. Each locality's pell-mell rush to profit and population fed on that of the others as the country was knitted together as never before, at least in the business of making and spending money. The later Laurier years saw a marked move towards large consolidated enterprises, with financing from the big banks, insurance firms and trust companies, often with assistance from outside capital. In the 1909-1911 period alone, the Canadian Cereal and Milling Company, Dominion Canners Limited, Dominion Steel Corporation, the British Columbia Packers Association, the Canada Bread Company, Sherwin Williams Company and the Canada Cement Company were formed, to name only leading examples. Probably the successful, or at any rate, energetic businessman should survive in the national memory as *the* Canadian of the period rather than Clifford Sifton's "stalwart peasant in a sheep-skin coat." In 1909, when the *Courier*, a popular magazine, polled readers as to "Canada's Ten Biggest Men," four of them were railway magnates, and of the next thirteen, five were industrialists or financiers. Business growth, to so many Canadians, was what real progress was

Widespread settlement and new provincial boundaries made it necessary to complete the series of western Indian land treaties, the first of which had been concluded in 1871. Commissioners Stewart and McMartin, here shown with their party, negotiated Treaty No. 9, which covered lands extending to Hudson and James bays, and included most of northern Ontario. It was signed on July 12, 1905.
Public Archives Canada, PA-59617.

all about. Right across the country, the development of national linkages among entrepreneurs, as well as those within professions such as the law, banking and engineering, went on at a great rate. By the late Laurier years Canada's allegedly vested interests were by no means wholly clustered around Toronto and Montreal. Boards of trade, bankers' associations, the Canadian Manufacturers' Association and all the other formal linkages were only the tip of the iceberg. The various groupings of the business elite, in different localities and sectors, freely pursued their countless rival interests, civic and corporate. But in their assumptions about how right and proper it was that *they*, and not the politicians, presided over and largely deserved the credit for the nation's prosperity and maturing, they were not divided. In 1891, the economic and power linkages associated with the National Policy's tariff protection and railways had been relatively weak, compared to what they would become in the Laurier period. Then this budding self-styled national class had been the backbone of continuing Conservative power. Now, ever so many of them were chummy with the Laurier Liberals, largely as a matter of profitability.

Canadian capitalism was increasingly involved in outside activities. Some of these entrepreneurs were so powerful, aggressive and ambitious that they played in the truly big leagues of business. For example, by the early 1900s men from Toronto and Montreal had big slices of tramway services and electric power generation in Brazil, Argentina, Mexico, Jamaica and Cuba. By 1905, the interest alone from these companies' securities was reported to have reached more than a million dollars yearly. Then too, there were the outside investments and enterprises in this country. Almost all of these were British and American. Most of the British money was in railroad and municipal bonds, purely as investment, while the U.S. capital sought and often achieved ownership of resources and factories. By 1912, American direct investment was over $400,000,000 and there were an estimated 209 American branch companies operating in Canada, far beyond the totals for British capital. Yet the London money market supplied almost three-quarters of Canadian borrowing by this time, New York less than 15 per cent.[5]

Even as times changed and new enterprises rose and fell in a vastly more wealthy and exciting economic environment, the long-standing Canadian fascination with railroads as the

OPPOSITE ABOVE
The following six paintings were executed between 1887, the year Laurier became Leader of the Opposition, and the turn of the century. They offer interesting contrasts to one another. Roper's view of the Fraser River near New Westminster, painted in 1887, is a late example of the documentary art that was giving way to photography; he was an English artist who had been sent to Canada to depict the western landscape for a magazine. Note that the river-side strollers include Chinese, who had come to the region in large numbers during the construction of the CPR. New Westminster, British Columbia, *by Edward Roper, 1887. Picture Division, Public Archives Canada, C-11035.*

OPPOSITE BELOW
Wayside sketching continued, but usually on a more personal basis. The attractive watercolour by Boultbee was painted in 1898, when he was struggling over the long portage between Telegraph Creek and Teslin Lake, bound for the Klondike gold fields. The contrast with Roper's realistic style is striking; Impressionist influence is evident.
Our Camp on the Mosquito River on the Trail from Telegraph Creek to Lake Teslin, *by A. E. Boultbee, 1898. Picture Division, Public Archives Canada, C-46598.*

HOMESTEADING IN SASKATCHEWAN.

A sod house on the prairie – the first home in the West for many farmer immigrants. *Public Archives Canada, PA-29090.*

key factor in material growth was stronger than ever. And it was in the railway field more than any other that the Laurier government, especially the Prime Minister himself, best seized the spirit of the age. Laurier was at the very height of his political career and national power in 1903-1904 as he presented his Grand Trunk Pacific-National Transcontinental railway policy to the country, and then won popular approval for it in his landslide federal election triumph of 1904.

Since the fiasco of Unrestricted Reciprocity in his opposition years, Laurier had not taken the lead for his Party on a detailed nuts-and-bolts material issue. Sifton in the interior department, Fielding in finance, Tarte in public works and Andrew Blair in the railways and canals portfolio were all more clearly associated in the public mind with such activities. But Laurier was a supremely sensitive political animal by now, and keenly felt the pressures and opportunities in the transportation issue in the early 1900s. In his own province of Quebec the dreams of priestly agricultural colonizers and of mining promoters centred on new trackage into the virtually deserted northwestern section of the province. Similar ambitions were

entertained in Ontario, whose Liberal Premier explained to Laurier: "It is of the greatest importance to Ontario that the area north of the C.P.R. should be opened up." He hoped for a new transcontinental railway that would "pass through probably 600 miles of New Ontario in a direct line nearly from east to west, traversing a fertile belt of about 16,000,000 acres, as well calculated for settlement as any part of Old Ontario." The Ontario government lines going into the region to open mining resources would conveniently intersect with such a transcontinental line. Many western farmers demanded alternative and competitive outlets to the CPR and service for the vast new regions far from its main lines. Then too, the ambitions of the Maritimes and the fortunes of their Liberals might improve if the all-season terminus of the new national line was situated there. On the other coast, development dreams in northern British Columbia could be played to by ending the line well to the north, just south of Alaska.

Laurier drew all these themes together and added a good many more in his stirring House of Commons speech of July 30, 1903 on the terms of charter for the new line. He unveiled the project as "a national as well as a commercial necessity." He spoke of the exploding wheat production in a West "invaded" by an immigrant flood which had reached 100,000 in 1902 and was still increasing; he referred to the desperate need for better marketing of Canadian industrial products, now increasing tremendously in volume. He strove to make the

The inauguration ceremonies of the Province of Saskatchewan, September 4, 1905. Sir Laurier and Lady Laurier joined Earl Grey and Lady Grey, Comr. A. B. Perry, Hon. Wm. Patterson, Sir Gilbert Parker and Lady Evelyn Grey among others.
Public Archives Canada, C-21896. Saskatchewan Archives Board photograph.

OPPOSITE
At this time Europe, and
in particular Paris, was the
Mecca of most Canadian
artists. Paul Peel, highly
accomplished but
academic and conventional,
spent most of his few
working years in France.
He died at 32. He had
left his country behind
him; there is nothing in his
work to suggest Canada.
The Little Shepherdess,
*by Paul Peel, 1892. Art
Gallery of Ontario.*

project less a railway than an enterprise of patriotism:

The flood of tide is upon us that leads on to fortune; if we
let it pass it may never recur again. If we let it pass, the
voyage of our national life, bright as it is today, will be
bound in shallows. We cannot wait, because time does not
wait; Heaven grant that it is not already too late; Heaven
grant that whilst we tarry and dispute, the trade of Canada
is not deviated to other channels, and that an ever vigilant
competitor does not take to himself the trade that properly
belongs to those who acknowledge Canada as their native
or their adopted land. Upon this question we feel that our
position is absolutely safe and secure; we feel that it cor-
responds to the beating of every Canadian heart.

By contrast, George A.
Reid, who also studied in
Paris, almost always represented Canadian subjects,
even when working
abroad. He lived until
1947, and during his long
life his work naturally
reflected changes in the
world of art. In the 1890s
he was the leading Cana-
dian genre painter of the
day. *Mortgaging the
Homestead*, a realistic
depiction of a family
crisis, reminds one of
Robert Harris's well-
known canvas, *A Meeting
of the School Trustees.
Mortgaging the Home-
stead, by George A. Reid,
1890. The National Gallery
of Canada, Ottawa. The
Royal Canadian Academy
of Arts, Diploma Work,
deposited 1891.*

The speed with which settlements could be established on the prairies, once transportation was available, was astonishing. The first train to reach the site of Kindersley, Saskatchewan (upper picture) arrived early in October 1909. By the time the lower picture was taken, only 35 days later, 150 buildings had been built. Kindersley was twice incorporated in 1910, first as a village and later as a town.
Canadian Annual Review, 1909. Metropolitan Toronto Library Board.

The government, he announced, would build a line from Moncton, New Brunswick to Winnipeg, the National Transcontinental, and then lease it to the Grand Trunk Pacific Co. free for seven years and then at three per cent of construction costs *per annum*. As a safeguard against default, the government would hold a first mortgage on the Company's property and rolling stock. The GTP would itself build, own and operate the western road, Winnipeg to the Pacific, but with federal aid. The government would guarantee 75 per cent of construction bonds up to $13,000 per mile through the prairies and $30,000 per mile in the mountains. When the road was completed, the GTP would provide rolling stock and would pay the three per cent interest charges on the mountain section after seven years — during which the government would cover them — and on the prairie section immediately. All told then, Laurier proclaimed, the total cost to the federal treasury, once the construction costs of the eastern section were reclaimed in rents, would be the seven years of interest on the mountain section — estimated at $13,000,000. He asked: "Now, Sir, what

is $13,000,000 in the year 1903?" With "a firm heart," he offered the people "a scheme worthy of this young nation for whom a heavy task has no terrors."

It *was* a heavy task, and there ought to have been *plenty* of terrors. The government-constructed eastern section was not completed until shortly before the outbreak of war in 1914, by which time costs had risen from the estimated $30,000 a mile to nearly $100,000 a mile. There had been understandable difficulties in running the line through the rock, forest and bog of northern Ontario and Quebec, but the grasping and graft of contractors and political hangers-on had contributed mightily to the soaring charges. Not unreasonably, the Grand Trunk Pacific was reluctant to take over its operation, with eventual liability for three per cent per year of the inflated costs. Its own western section, a brilliantly constructed line from an engineering point of view, also had cost far more than expected, and by 1912 overseas capital was becoming harder to find in sufficient amounts. Taken together, the two sections had too many desolate stretches of territory which would take decades to produce profitable traffic. Then too, there was the astonishing fact that in these years of boundless confidence and foolish finance the new line had to face com-

Many immigrants came to the Canadian West from the United States. Mr. and Mrs. Tom Ogden were en route from Boston to Alberta in the spring of 1910.
Public Archives Canada, C-37963. Glenbow-Alberta Institute, Calgary, Alberta.

petition in the most profitable regions from not only the established CPR, but also the expanding Canadian Northern empire of William Mackenzie and Donald Mann.

Mackenzie and Mann, both Ontario born, had battled their way to prominence through clever financial, railway and tramway deals in Canada and abroad. In the mid-1890s they had joined forces to take control of a Manitoba railway, which became the basis for their sprawling western network, honeycombing the prairies and reaching into British Columbia. They specialized in buying up old franchises with their attached land grants, winning municipal and provincial subsidies and bond guarantees, and convincing the usually wary British investors that substantial profits were a virtual certainty in their clever though unorthodox operations. Substantial public support was won in the West through reasonable rates and customer-oriented service, made feasible by cut-rate costs on construction and equipment. By 1901 the cocky, tough, barrel chested Mann and the slim, intense Mackenzie were ready to go transcontinental. It made obvious economic sense for the western based Canadian Northern to coalesce, or at least co-operate, with the old eastern based Grand Trunk, but the Grand Trunk distrusted the "new boys," their methods and their motives; and so did Sir Wilfrid Laurier. The Prime Minister also seemed to have believed that the boom times would go on and on indefinitely — hence there would be enough business for more than one new system. Besides, as Mann told a Quebec *Chronicle* reporter, he and his partner were not interested:

> We will have nothing to do with the Grand Trunk people. What is more, we have no need of them. We control 85 per cent of the stock of our railway and we mean to hold on to our property and manage it ourselves. We have 1,200 miles of road finished and running. We are making a large profit with a surplus of over $600,000 per year over running expenses, besides paying interest on all monies borrowed.

They continued to build up their western trackage as settlement progressed, hoping thus to gain the financial and traffic basis for their eastern extensions. By 1911, the originally unsympathetic Laurier government in Ottawa, under western pressure, guaranteed $39,000,000 of the securities on their Montreal to Port Arthur section.

OPPOSITE
Harris himself, best known as the painter of the famous picture of the Fathers of Confederation, painted this fine portrait of Sir Oliver Mowat in 1892. Very appropriately, it now hangs in the Parliament Buildings in Toronto, for Mowat was Premier of Ontario for 24 years. In 1896 Laurier persuaded him to leave provincial politics and join his Cabinet as Minister of Justice.
Portrait of Oliver Mowat by Robert Harris, 1892. Government of Ontario Art Collection. Photography: Jim Chambers.

Some of the new western communities reflected the regions from which settlers had come. The Thunder Hill Colony in Manitoba, built by Doukhobors, bore a strong resemblance to the villages they had left behind in Russia.
Public Archives Canada, C-683.

The eventual collapse of both the Grand Trunk Pacific-National Transcontinental and the Canadian Northern, their incorporation into the federally owned Canadian National Railways, and that public system's normally unprofitable state thereafter were not developments of the Laurier years. But they clearly were a legacy of Sir Wilfrid's policies. The full combination of adverse circumstances — the spiralling construction costs, the economic pauses of 1907 and 1913, and the drying up of the vital London capital supplies and immigration flow which World War I brought about — hardly could have been foreseen in 1903 and 1904. The fact remains, however, that very soon after Laurier left office and before most of these occurrences had taken place, the serious weaknesses of his transcontinental railways policies were clear enough, especially to his successors in power at Ottawa. In July 1912, the Grand Trunk Pacific, fearing heavier burdens than it could afford, began to press the government to release it from its obligation to assume operation of the eastern National Transcontinental. In 1913 the GTP begged a $15,000,000 loan from the federal authorities, and in 1914 a guarantee of principal and interest on $16,000,000 worth of the railway's bonds. A price of the second assistance was the government's assumption of mortgage rights on the railway's own western section. The Canadian Northern was no less sickly and just as much a drain on federal finances. A loan of $5,000,000 was granted it in 1912; in January 1913 another for $15,000,000 was authorized in return for $7,000,000 worth of the corporation's common stock. A year later, Mackenzie and Mann were back, begging a loan or other aid to prevent default on their debt payments. Borden was warned of disastrous implications for several provinces and financial institutions if the collapse were permitted to happen. Reluctantly, he gave a federal guarantee for $45,000,000 of Canadian Northern bonds, in return for additional railway stock, bringing the government's share in ownership to a level of 40 per cent. This lavish public aid was enough to complete the two lines in 1915, but they could not survive the special financial and traffic problems of wartime. Additional millions of government funding kept them going while the nationalization process went forward, to be completed soon after War's end. In 1919, Arthur Meighen, the federal minister

A Doukhobor harness shop in Ooteshenie, B.C. *Provincial Archives, Victoria, B.C.*

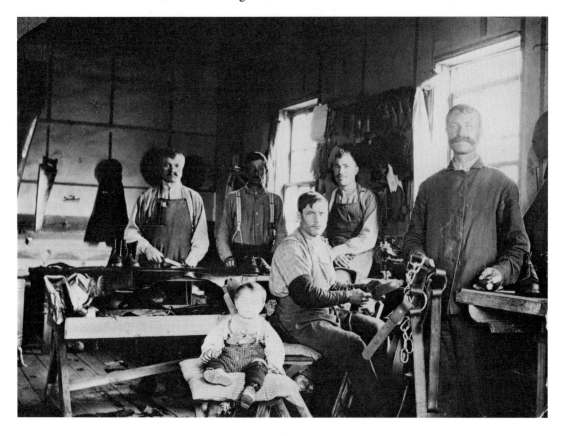

THE CANADIAN PACIFIC RAILWAY
DINING CARS
Excel in Elegance of Design and Furniture
AND IN THE
Quality of Food and Attendance
ANYTHING HITHERTO OFFERED TO
TRANSCONTINENTAL TRAVELLERS.

The fare provided is the best procurable, and the cooking has a wide reputation for excellence. Local delicacies, such as trout, prairie hens, antelope steaks, Fraser River salmon, succeed one another as the train moves westward.

The wines are of the Company's special importation, and are of the finest quality.

These cars accompany all transcontinental trains, and are managed directly by the Railway Company, which seeks, as with its hotels and sleeping cars, to provide every comfort and luxury without regard to cost—looking to the general profit of the Railway rather than to the immediate returns from these branches of its service

who superintended the last stages of the takeover, made a bitter comment:

> We are at the penalty stage of railway development in this country; a price in some form has to be paid by the people of Canada. We are at the point now where an awakening of bitterness follows a night of intoxication; an ebb of retribution now follows in the wake of a flood tide of railway construction.[6]

It is undeniable that Laurier, more than any other Canadian, was responsible for the over-optimistic over-building of the railways. His inability or unwillingness to force the Grand Trunk and Canadian Northern to merge their transcontinental activities and ambitions — as Clifford Sifton had urged — was a major contributing factor to the eventual disaster. Even Robert Borden's alternative of national ownership of *one* new transcontinental would have made much more sense. In the most significant domestic economic project of his career, Laurier preferred to follow his political instincts, playing dramatically to a host of regional ambitions and dreams, and with an eye on his immediate electoral prospects. The sweeping Liberal victory of 1904 showed that prudence and caution were unpopular, even "un-Canadian," when the crucial deci-

De luxe travel at the turn of the century: a Canada Atlantic Railway parlour car about 1900.
Public Archives Canada, C-25966.

OPPOSITE
From *The New West Extending from the Great Lakes across Plain and Mountain to the Golden Shores of the Pacific,* Canadian Historical Publishing Co., 1888. *Metropolitan Toronto Library Board.*

Issued Twice, April, 1907

EXCURSIONS

SETTLERS'

One Way Excursions

Every Tuesday
in April, 1907

From St. Paul, Minneapolis, Duluth
and Points East and South

to all points on

CANADIAN NORTHERN RY.

Write R. CREELMAN, T. P. A., 166 East Third Street, St. Paul,
for Settlers' Folder

HOMESEEKERS'

Round Trip Excursions
To all points on Canadian Northern Railway

Every Tuesday
in April, 1907
ONE FARE PLUS $2.00

From St. Paul, Minneapolis, Duluth
and Points East and South

First Class   Stop-overs   Limit 21 Days

3

sions were being made. The temper of the times was never better illustrated than in the advice of Joseph Flavelle, a Toronto entrepreneur, to a friend in 1903:

Men who have studied about older communities, who have fixed their ideas of economic questions on old world conditions, who have developed their theories from contact with long established and somewhat inflexible relations, cannot easily realize how entirely different are the problems confronting this young and undeveloped country. All sorts of mistakes can be made — doubtless will be made. All sorts of errors of judgment, mistaken expenditures, extravagant policies, will be present; and yet the great productive power of her yet unbroken prairie lands, her uncut forests, her undeveloped mines, her exhaustless fisheries, will produce such an amount of wealth year by year that will quite override these unfavourable circumstances.[7]

That indeed may have been what happened, in the longest perspective. Undoubtedly, in spite of many false starts and disappointments, the spread of settlement, the exploitation of natural resources and the consolidation of markets now went ahead at a faster rate, at least in part because of the accelerated railway building. The country's various isolated regions and communities were brought closer together, in enterprise and

Luxury hotels built to accommodate rising numbers of tourists were part of the Canadian Pacific Railway travel empire. The Chateau Frontenac overlooking the St. Lawrence River at Quebec, and the Banff Hotel in the Rockies (shown here) were two spectacular additions to the C.P.R. list of offerings.
Public Archives Canada, PA-31580.

in spirit. Most of the gains, however, could have been secured by a less reckless, less political policy. Then the burdens on the nation's future finances and the disillusionment of localities and regions whose promised golden age never came would not have been so severe.

The hustle and bustle of a highly materialistic time could be very disconcerting, if one was looking for signs of greater "civilization," of a growth in cultural maturity. "My American friends were full of kindly scorn when I announced that I was going to Canada," wrote Rupert Brooke, the English poet. " 'A country without a soul!' they cried, and pressed books upon me, to befriend me through that Philistine bleakness."[8] It was undeniable that there was a great deal of the rough and ready in a land growing so fast and among people so devoted to the pursuit of material gain and to the accumulation of power. Summing up the period, W. S. Milner, a writer in the ambitious multi-volume *Canada and its Provinces*, published

Sir Wilfrid and Lady Laurier en route to a Parliamentary luncheon during the Colonial Conference in London, 1907. Always clothes-conscious, the two were an eye-catching couple. *Public Archives Canada, C-33388.*

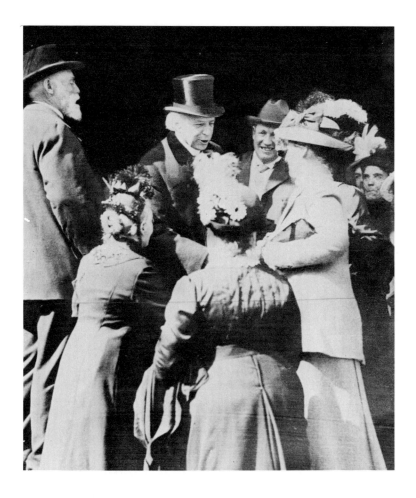

in 1914, before setting forth evidence of the country's cultural advance, remarked: "Our fundamental problem is . . . the problem of a commercial democracy feverishly busy in the development of half a continent."

A glimpse of Sir Wilfrid campaigning during the general election of 1908. *Public Archives Canada,* C-932.

Nevertheless, considerable progress did take place in a host of cultural and intellectual fields in the Laurier "boom" years. The older universities expanded in size and took on new functions. On the prairies new and impressive universities blossomed. Opportunities abounded for engineers and architects, in connection with the vast new public projects as well as the magnificent private homes of the leaders of enterprise and the professions. The Royal Society of Canada played an invigorated role in the stimulation of cultural and scientific activity, matching the heightened sophistication in the universities. Not surprisingly in a country so involved in traversing

Laurier speaking at an outdoor Liberal election rally in Berlin (now Kitchener) in 1908. Before the days of loudspeakers, the strain on a politician's voice at large gatherings was intense.
Public Archives Canada, C-463.

vast distances through rugged terrain, and in extracting its resources, advances in the geological sciences were particularly impressive. Similarly, agricultural science thrived on the challenges inherent in northern settlement. The *Queen's Quarterly*, dating from 1893, and the *University Magazine*, begun in 1907 and sponsored by McGill, Dalhousie and the University of Toronto, were signs of the growth of a general intellectual confidence and activity, even if many of the academic and literary contributors sometimes despaired of the "parvenu" society around them. On a broader basis, the highly successful

OPPOSITE

The writings of four poets who had won distinction in pre-Laurier days continued to dominate the Canadian literary scene during the first decade of the new century. Charles G. D. Roberts and Bliss Carman were New Brunswick-born cousins; Duncan Campbell Scott and Archibald Lampman were born in Ontario. Lorne Pierce noted the interrelations that linked them: "Bliss Carman . . . derived encouragement from Roberts' success and stimulation from his companionship. Roberts' *Orion* also kindled Archibald Lampman, and Lampman fired the latent genius of Duncan Campbell Scott, and so on the impulse went." On a more popular level the writings of Robert W. Service, "the poet of the Yukon," whose first book *Songs of a Sourdough*, appeared in 1907, met with great success.

Sir Charles G. D. Roberts.
Public Archives Canada,
C-6718.

Bliss Carman.
The Dominion Illustrated,
1891. Public Archives
Canada, C-25816.

Duncan Campbell Scott.
Public Archives Canada,
C-3187.

Archibald Lampman.
Public Archives Canada,
C-68854.

Robert Service (back row, right) photographed in Dawson with a group of friends celebrating the publication of *Songs of a Sourdough*.

"Canadian Club" movement grew with astonishing speed in the early years of the century, to become, as one writer of the time put it, "a very remarkable instrument for the diffusion of intelligent opinion throughout the whole country."

It was the country itself which was the focus of some of the most exciting and fruitful cultural achievements. Historians and novelists were finding new popularity, at home and abroad. But much of what they did, in English and French, was still kept mediocre by romantic conventions or religious sanctions. It was in English language poetry and in painting generally that the confidence, maturity and self-assurance of Laurier's Canada found their most satisfactory manifestations.

"The chief glory of Canadian literature is its poetry," wrote T. G. Marquis in 1914. Premier place was deserved by a quite distinguished little group: Archibald Lampman, Duncan Campbell Scott and Wilfred Campbell from Ontario, with Charles G. D. Roberts and Bliss Carman from New Brunswick. Roberts first published significant verse in 1880, and practically all these men were making names for themselves in the later 1880s and early 1890s. But it was at the dawn and in the first decade of the new century that they spoke with special maturity and grace to a wider and more appreciative audience. Probably Roberts had most to do with touching off their explosion of energy and excellence. Archibald Lampman was a Trinity College undergraduate in the early 1880s when he read Roberts' *Orion and Other Poems* (1880), published when the author was only twenty. Lampman wrote:

I sat up most of the night reading and re-reading *Orion* in a state of the wildest excitement and when I went to bed I could not sleep. It seemed to me a wonderful thing that such a work could be done by a Canadian, by a young man, one of ourselves. It was like a voice from some new paradise of art, calling us to be up and doing.

Roberts drew his cousin Bliss Carman into a literary career; and as editor of *The Week* in Toronto in the 1880s he vigorously promoted the early poems of Lampman and Carman. Then Lampman, Duncan Campbell Scott and Wilfred Campbell came together in the federal civil service, and, in 1892-93, they collaborated on a charming column of literary *causerie* and verse in the Toronto *Globe*. By no means a formal set, the five were yet of a generation, sharing much.

 Foremost among the common threads was a sensitive celebration of the Canadian environment. In their best work these poets evoked the loneliness, the panorama, the contrasts of the seasons in colours and moods, and the stimulation of the northern landscape. It was far more in this manner than in explicit hymning of nationhood itself that they expressed their unapologetic love of country. Lampman's sonnet "In the Wilds," published after his death, at the age of 38 in 1899, was a particularly striking example:

> The Methodist Book and Publishing House, here advertising the "Poet of the Yukon," was later to become The Ryerson Press, one of the most influential publishers in the history of Canadian letters.
> Canadian Annual Review, 1908. *Metropolitan Toronto Library Board.*

We run with rushing streams that toss and spume:
We speed or dream upon the open meres;
The pine woods fold us in their pungent gloom;
The thunder of wild water fills our ears;
The rain we take, we take the beating sun;
The stars are cold above our heads at night;
On the rough earth we lie when day is done
And slumber even in the storm's despite.

The savage vigour of the forest creeps
Into our veins, and laughs upon our lips;
The warm blood kindles from forgotten deeps,
And surges tingling to the finger tips.
The deep-pent life awakes and bursts its bands:
We feel the strength and goodness of our hands.

The beauty of the bitter northern winter also enthused him, as the last three lines of "Winter Uplands" attest:

... And then the golden moon to light me home —
The crunching snowshoes and the stinging air,
And silence, frost and beauty everywhere.

This was reminiscent of an earlier poem of Wilfred Campbell, "How One Winter Came in the Lake Region," ending:

That night I felt the winter in my veins
A joyous tremour of the icy glow;
And woke to hear the north's wild vibrant strains,
While far and wide, by withered woods and plains,
Fast fell the driving snow.

Bliss Carman, in a Maritimes setting, also was evoking in these years themes about the Canadian environment, with a unique sort of emotionalism, as in "Low Tide on Grand Pré":

... Was it a year or lives ago
We took the grasses in our hands,
And caught the summer flying low
Over the waving meadow lands,
And held it there between our hands? ...

The night has fallen, and the tide ...
Now and again comes drifting home,
Across these aching barrens wide,
A sigh like driven wind or foam:
In grief the flood is bursting home.

This generation of poets, of which any nation could be proud, had reached maturity by or in the Laurier years. In the quality of their best verse and in the international recognition which it received, they signalled to Canadians that the grip of cultural provincialism had been loosened, perhaps even that it could be broken. Their successors could not ignore the

Stephen Leacock,
Canada's leading
humourist, published his
first books, *Literary
Lapses* and *Nonsense
Novels*, in the last years of
Laurier's term in office.
Public Archives Canada,
C-5480.

urban, industrial, and socially divided country where most
Canadians would be forced to live, divorced from all but limited familiarity with nature. The tradition of excellence and
confidence would remain, however, as would the heritage of
loving contemplation of the country's variety and vastness.

Canadian painters moved steadily in these years to a similar
fascination with and love for the northern environment.[9] Some,
led by Maurice Cullen, James Wilson Morrice, Clarence
Gagnon and Marc Aurèle de Foy Suzor-Côté, drew on excellent training in Europe, especially picking up approaches
from the French impressionist tradition. Cullen in *Logging in
Winter, Beaupré* (1896) worked wonders with the varied
colours of snow in bright northern sunlight and forest shadows.
That painting, and canvases of Montreal winter streets and

isolated Laurentian scenes, prompted Morrice's words in 1910 that Cullen was "the man in Canada who gets at the guts of things." Morrice took a similar approach, favouring what he called "healthy, lusty colour" over the traditionally popular "pale Dutch monochromes." As E. F. B. Johnson would write in *Canada and its Provinces*:

> The brightness and clearness of physical Canada and the ex-
> ternals of the life of its people must indicate the character
> of the artist's expression. A picture full of that atmosphere
> which dominates the works of the Dutch masters would be
> wanting in truth as applied to Canada, and when it is urged
> that Canadian works of art are hard and more or less realistic,
> it should not be forgotten that the artist must paint the coun-
> try as he finds it, and not as he might wish to make it.

It was significant that so many Canadian artists were confidently taking this sort of approach, notwithstanding criticisms, at home and abroad, from so-called cosmopolitans.
Morrice produced some evocative depictions of Quebec City
and of the life and scenery of the province's countryside.
Clarence A. Gagnon made winter scenes in Quebec countryside and town his speciality, and Suzor-Côté excelled with
vivid portraits of habitant life and personalities.

Among the artists whose lack of European grounding did
not prevent work of distinction were Homer Watson and
Horatio Walker, both from rural Ontario. Well into maturity
and popularity by the turn of the century, they captured the
tone of farm life, Watson in his native Grand River valley and
Walker on the Ile d'Orléans, near Quebec City.

Thus, when some of the artists who later would inspire
or originate the Group of Seven were beginning their careers
in the years just before 1911, a tradition of confident Canadian
landscape painting was already in existence. As the talented
Torontonian, Charles W. Jefferys, declared: "It is inevitable
that a country with such marked physical characteristics as
Canada possesses should impress itself forcefully upon our
artists." His *Western Sunlight, Lost Mountain Lake* (1911)
communicated the beauty of yet another Canadian environment. That same year, Jefferys, in turn, was very struck by
some Northern Ontario sketches of the young J. E. H. Mac-
Donald, remarking: "Mr. MacDonald's art is native — as native

as the rocks, or the snow, or pine trees, or the lumber drives that are so largely his themes." MacDonald, Tom Thomson, Arthur Lismer and Frank Carmichael already were working and sketching together, and associations with Lawren Harris and A. Y. Jackson would occur very soon. In British Columbia, Emily Carr was beginning to blend her love of the life, religious mysticism and art of coastal Indian villages with the vivid Fauve colouring she had picked up in Europe. The effect would be dramatic, emotional and *very* Canadian.

During these years Homer Watson, a landscape painter, was probably the best known of Canadian artists. He studied abroad, but found almost all his subjects in the Grand River Valley, Ontario, where he was born and lived almost the whole of his long life. The influence of Constable was evident in his work at this time, but *The Flood Gate* is the only painting in which he himself admitted to having imitated him. Later, Watson's work became less romantic and more clearly identifiable with the Canadian scene. *The Flood Gate, by Homer Watson, 1900. The National Gallery of Canada, Ottawa.*

In numerous features of life then, Canada by the late Laurier years was a society of confidence. We shall see that millions of Canadians did not really share in the prosperity of the time nor in the sense of assurance of great achievements and rewards to come. Nevertheless, this was an era when it truthfully could be said that "the land is strong," at least for those persons, now significantly increased in numbers and scope of activity, who were pushing back the frontiers of achievement, whether in enterprise or in cultural life. The country's roots were being driven deeper into the soil, and the doubts and hesitations about the national future which had been so common in the 1880s and early 1890s were now increasingly hard to find, at least at any levels of effective power and influence.

4
Problems in
Paradise

In 1908, a young Methodist minister and settlement worker in Winnipeg, James Shaver Woodsworth, surveyed the social environment in his city, with its quickened industrialization and incredible intake of immigrant labour, and remarked: "True prosperity cannot be measured by the volume of trade and bank clearings. It consists in the social and moral welfare of the people." As a mission worker in a city settlement, he was deeply concerned by the often horrible working and living conditions which oppressed so many immigrants and workers.

An old-style composing room at Brampton, Ontario in 1905. Much of the typesetting was still done by hand.
Metropolitan Toronto Library Board.

No doubt Laurier had cause to take pride in the extent and tempo of the material growth which typified his years of office. But the social problems related to mass industrialization were not a sphere in which he moved comfortably or confidently. What was more, his *laissez faire* principles and provincial rights habits of thought did not incline him towards any serious intervention by his government in the marketplace economy which spawned the problems. Likewise, while he had a right to boast about the successes of his immigration policy, he and other political leaders eventually had to face the growing antipathy of many native Canadians, worried about both job security and cultural integrity, towards the people Woods-

The following six paintings were executed during the years of Laurier's prime ministry. These years saw the emergence of the first Canadian painter of international stature — Montreal-born James Wilson Morrice. Though he spent much of his life in Paris, and painted also in Italy, North Africa and the West Indies, Morrice paid frequent visits to Canada and found many of his best known subjects in Quebec. Whistler, Matisse and other painters of the day influenced him, but his style always had individuality. *Return from School* was painted in the early 1900s; *The Ferry, Quebec*, a famous canvas, in 1909.
James Wilson Morrice: Return from School, *c. 1900 (Art Gallery of Ontario) and* The Ferry, Quebec, *c. 1909 (The National Gallery of Canada, Ottawa).*

worth called "strangers within our gates." The Prime Minister's expertise in solving the problems of an older, quieter, more agrarian, more Anglo-French Canada, were not of much help when he was obliged to try and meet these new challenges. There were, of course, constitutional limits as to what a federal government could do in these social fields. Whatever the reasons, Laurier and his government seemed increasingly ineffectual to important segments of the population who were given little reason to suppose that their national government really knew how they lived, cared about their problems, or sympathized with their concerns.

Wherever the impact of the Laurier boom was felt in urban Canada, poverty followed close behind. Slum conditions were nothing new, but their intensity in the midst of the new plenty could be unsettling. In 1897, a reform-minded Montrealer, Herbert Ames, wrote *A City Below the Hill*, a study of the tenement districts stretching from the foot of the mountain to the river. This and other sources revealed that the death rate for the city as a whole in 1895 was 24.81 per thousand, higher than for London, Paris, Rome, Boston or New York, not to mention all other Canadian cities. In the worst sections of town it was as high as 35. An unfiltered water system, lax supervision of the unpasteurized milk supply and widespread use of outdoor toilets, crowded together in postage stamp yards, were only some of the reasons for the alarming statistics. Gastroenteric diseases were rife, especially in infants and small children. Between 1899 and 1901 26.8 per cent of all babies died before reaching the age of one, a proportion more than twice that of New York. Meanwhile, the middle-class-dominated city and provincial governments spent only tiny amounts on public health, welfare and education, leaving private charities a mighty gap to fill, rarely with noticeable success at rescuing people from the state of poverty.[1]

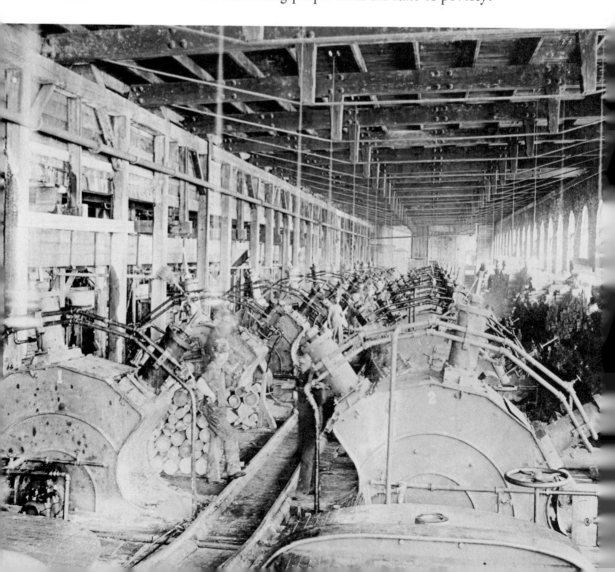

The grinding room in the pulp mills at Sault Ste. Marie, Ontario, about 1900 when the pulp and paper industry was developing on a substantial scale. Output would increase from about $8 million in 1901 to over $100 million by the time of Laurier's death in 1919. *Public Archives Canada, PA-52774.*

Social workers and reformers in all the major Canadian cities called attention to this developing urban crisis. In Toronto, as the first decade of the new century drew to a close, the Rev. H. H. Magee denounced what he saw as the criminal carelessness which allowed deplorable housing conditions to exist. Miss Charity Cook, a social worker, recorded some details in 1909:

A 1907 Toronto Niagara Power Company crew erects poles for a 12,000-volt line.
Ontario Hydro.

> Our work is all among the poor, and only yesterday one of our workers went to a home where father, mother and five children were living in two rooms. One child was tubercular. They were sleeping four in one bed, and the sick child on a couch...
>
> We have one family not far from our mission where the woman drinks and is thoroughly immoral. She has a little boy about ten years of age threatened with tuberculosis. He was in the hospital and they said his only chance was good nourishment, the best of care and lots of fresh air, but in this place there is no possible ventilation... We come across so much of that kind of thing in our work, and yet people cannot believe that such a state of affairs exists in Toronto.

Maurice Cullen, an Impressionist, was born in Newfoundland but grew up in Montreal. He was a close friend of Morrice, and they painted together in France, Italy and Quebec. *The Old Ferry* has much in common with the Morrice canvas. The best of Cullen's landscapes, street scenes and harbour views rank very high indeed in the whole range of Canadian painting. The Old Ferry, Louise Basin, Quebec, *by Maurice Cullen, 1907. The National Gallery of Canada, Ottawa.*

Toronto's population surge could not be accommodated in decent new housing at prices the lower income workers could afford. Consequently, the decaying older neighbourhoods degenerated rapidly into tenement districts, in which, according to a relief officer in 1904, "there is scarcely a . . . home fit to live in that is not inhabited, and in many cases by numerous families; in fact, . . . respectable people have had to live in stables, tents, old cars, sheds (others in damp cellars), where we would not place a valued animal, let alone a human being."[2]

Winnipeg, supposedly the success city of the era, had its festering social sores too. Here in particular, class and ethnic divisions tended to coincide. The well-to-do of the South End and the prosperous middle class and skilled working class of the West End and central city — mostly Anglo-Saxon — were separated physically and socially by the CPR tracks and the railway's mammoth yards from the low income, mostly unskilled, largely immigrant working class of the North End.[3] J. S. Woodsworth, at the All People's Mission in the North End, in 1911 published a book about his experiences entitled *My Neighbour*. He believed that poverty in the midst of Canadian plenty had a simple cause: the low wages paid by employers whose spiralling profits were not being passed on to a much too large labour force. It was a buyer's market in labour, and this economic fact had tragic social consequences:

How then keep up a home, as many are forced to do, on much less than the minimum $900?

Often this can be done by the ordinary family income being supplemented by the earnings of the wife and children, and this, alas, too often means the sacrifice of the best things that home life should yield.

When the mother is absent from the home the children are sadly neglected. The younger children suffer physically; the older ones through lack of discipline often become utterly unmanageable and thus qualify for a life of crime.

. . . Often children are kept from school and set to work at a very young age. Frequently health is impaired, morals corrupted and educational opportunities forever lost.

The same problem of insufficient income for the working class was at the heart of Montreal's poverty problems. Seasonal unemployment and the steady influx of immigrants and off-the-farm labourers prepared to work for next to nothing kept

Boom of logs and a sawmill at Chatham, New Brunswick. This scene could have been matched at many other points along both the Atlantic and Pacific coasts in Laurier's day.
The Wood Industries of Canada, 1897. *Public Archives Canada, C-29904.*

wages very low and trade unionism almost nonexistent. To keep family incomes even fairly adequate, women and children took employment, however low paid. Women made up 20 per cent of the labour force in 1896, and children 4 per cent. These percentages rose sharply as so-called boom conditions brought increased and serious inflation, at and after the turn of the century. The public school system, especially that serving the mostly French-speaking Roman Catholics, were too poor, pedagogically and financially, to constitute much of a

An old-time bunkhouse, still the sort of living quarters provided for miners and lumber camp workers in the Laurier era. *Public Archives Canada, C-38620.*

countervailing influence to child labour, especially in the absence of compulsory attendance laws.[4]

Wherever Canadians worked in unskilled or semi-skilled labouring or menial jobs, subsistence living in normal times could become an experience in severe hardship during recessions, as in 1907-1908. One example at that time concerned men employed at the Dominion Textile Company in Montreal. Wages were paid on an hourly rate, and distress mounted through the winter as hours of work were cut back drastically. In the spring of 1908 the wage rate itself was cut by 10 per cent. The men struck, but to no avail. Some idea of how little the wage earner in Canada was sharing in the prosperity of the period can be gained from official federal government figures covering an index of average weekly wage rates and family budget costs in thirteen Canadian cities (1913 = 100).

	Weekly Wage	Family Budget
1901	69.8	69.7
1911	92.4	92.7

In the Canada of Laurier's time, assistance for the needy had to come largely from local and provincial governments. Some progress was made during the early years of the century in improving education, health standards, the availability of public housing, workmen's compensation and pension protection, parks and so on. So-called reform administrations took control of several cities and self-styled progressive governments operated in a number of provinces, experimenting with regulation and even public ownership of key services. Typical of the new style was J. P. Whitney, the Conservative Premier of Ontario from 1905 to 1914, under whom Ontario Hydro was created and major advances made in the fields of industrial safety and technical training.

Federal activity in the fields of social welfare and public ownership of utilities was almost nonexistent, but the building of a modest base from which future growth might be possible began in 1909 with the creation of the Canadian Commission of Conservation under Laurier's former Minister of the Interior, Clifford Sifton. Though federally funded, it included representatives of the provinces, which had primary responsibility in the resources field. But the Commission did not re-

Cullen's influence was felt by many other painters, A. Y. Jackson amongst them. Jackson's name is so closely associated with the famous Group of Seven that it is often forgotten that he was painting long before the Group came into being in 1920. He managed to travel to Europe, where like many others he was converted to Impressionism. *Early Spring* was painted early in 1905; Jackson was to live until 1974, working almost to the last. *The Edge of the Maple Wood*, a semi-impressionist painting executed in 1910, has a special interest because it caught the attention of Lawren Harris and led to the association between the two that continued for many years.

A. Y. Jackson: Early Spring, Hemingford, *1905 (Art Gallery of Ontario) and* The Edge of the Maple Wood, *1910 (The National Gallery of Canada, Ottawa).*

strict its studies and research to nonurban matters, taking up questions of public health, town planning and housing as well. Though only an advisory body, it was a step at least towards the federal intervention in social concerns which would be so central a feature of Canadian life in later years. But, at the time, the various leaders of both the national parties, and the great bulk of their active followers, were not prepared to take really serious action towards redistributing income or power, thus leaving corporations and the wealthy to be the true leaders and beneficiaries of the national success. There was simply not the social or political strength yet present for any other result. It was not yet apparent to many middle-class Canadians, for most of whom life had never before been so rewarding or enjoyable, that widespread destitution, or close to it, for vast numbers of their fellow citizens was incompatible with long-run social stability. A governing party of supposedly liberal character could not long thrive in such circumstances.

The Laurier government's labour policy from 1896 to 1911 was a case in point. On the surface, it could be said that much was accomplished: the Department of Labour was set up in 1900 (and was to become a separate portfolio nine years later); and major legislation was enacted concerning conciliation and arbitration of a broad range of labour disputes. What

Industries can continue to grow while methods and sources of supply change. The last of the thousands of timber rafts that came down the Ottawa River was photographed in 1908, with the Parliament Buildings in the background.
Public Archives Canada, C-5068.

was more, William Lyon Mackenzie King, a qualified expert, trained at the highest university and social settlement centres in Canada, the United States and Britain, was prominently involved in these activities, as deputy minister and then minister in the new department. But appearances were not everything: when the government left office in 1911 the wage and organizational positions of trade unionists across Canada had been improved only slightly, if at all; and much of organized labour was openly hostile to the Liberals and opposed to their policies.

It was not so in the beginning. From the late 1880s the Liberals had drawn greater unionist support than their Conservative opponents. The former Tory leanings of many skilled craft unionists in the 1870s, when Macdonald's Trade Unions Act had safeguarded their legal right to exist, had been eroded in the depressed times of the 1880s, especially when the manufacturer-dominated Conservatives at Ottawa declined to pass demanded factory legislation. Meanwhile, modestly pro-labour moves by some provincial Liberal administrations did not pass unnoticed. In Ontario, Oliver Mowat's Factory Act of 1884 authorized regulations against unsafe conditions, excessive hours and the exploitation of women and children in the work force. Mowat himself was a cabinet minister in the early days of the Laurier government, and a colleague, William Mulock, M.P. from West Toronto and new Postmaster General, had received particularly strong support from working men in his election.

It was Mulock who brought Mackenzie King into the centre of Liberal policy making in the labour field. King was a chubby faced 23-year-old, and mid way through his post-graduate training, in the summer of 1897, when he prepared a series of articles for the Toronto *Mail and Empire* on some of the Queen City's social problems, particularly that of "sweated" or unregulated contract labour in the clothing industry. He was an emotional humanitarian properly shocked at what he discovered. In his diary, he wrote: "What a story of Hell. My mind all ablaze," and, "Oh such work & no pay, no reward — I felt in church as though I were worshipping with parasites, so much need outside in the sweat shop." Soon after, he went with his father to call on William Mulock, a family friend, with a triumphant diary entry being the result:

Mackenzie King in 1900 when he joined the civil service as first editor of the *Labour Gazette*. Within a few months, he advanced to the rank of Deputy Minister of Labour.
Public Archives Canada, PA-25941.

> I had a talk with him on economic questions & particularly the sweating system. I left with father & then went back to speak of the manffr. [manufacture] of clothing for militia etc. & told him I was going to protest against old methods. We then had a long talk & he offered to put in force any practical remedy I would suggest. Later he sd. he would appoint me to conduct an investigation in past abuses & frame measures of reform. . . . He is anxious to effect reform. Told me what he had done so far re contracts & what he wd. do in consequence of our conversat'n. He wd. not have thought of the matter but for our talk. . . . It was [means?] that I make a definite stand on the side of labour, as it involves the showing up of corrupt'n & robbery by wealthy men. I will only have the truth no matter what the cost.[5]

The words bespoke the spirit of the muckraking "progressivism" then beginning to come into vogue in the United States, and the young King did not exaggerate their effect on

William Mulock. The minister announced almost at once that contracts with his own department, the Post Office, henceforth would contain clauses to prevent sub-contracting and to ensure proper sanitary conditions, wages and hours of work. Shortly thereafter, the Prime Minister himself pledged that this principle would be "extended to every department of the Government." Fair Wage schedules for various regions were soon prepared. By 1910, seven provinces and 42 municipalities had chosen to undertake similar programs. Doubtless, the federal initiatives were not solely the result of King's representation — in particular, a by-election was under way in 1897 in generally

Tory Toronto and the government craved labour support. But whatever the motivation these were brave beginnings for the government in the labour field.

Additional steps were not long in coming. To oversee the anti-sweating regulations and to provide accurate data on which to base them, a Fair Wages bureau was established under Mulock, and this became the germ of the Department of Labour. Mackenzie King was snatched from Harvard to be the first deputy minister and to direct publication of *The Labour Gazette*, in which appeared each month factual information on labour conditions, legislation, contracts and strikes

Fishermen, their schooners, and gear; Souris, P.E.I., c. 1910. Although increased industrialization was changing the nature of economic life in the Maritime Provinces of Laurier's day, the traditional importance of the fishing trade was not lost. Notman Photographic Archives, McCord Museum of McGill University.

throughout the country. King maintained that the *Gazette* was "not sent out in the interest of any special class but for the good of the industrial community as a whole." The Canadian Manufacturers' Association publication, *Industrial Canada*, was highly suspicious nonetheless, objecting especially to the appointment of union partisans to posts within the department and with the *Gazette*. By the end of the Laurier years, the department was assembling detailed reports as well on cost-of-living figures, an essential statistical basis for any intelligently conceived future social welfare legislation.

The department's major activity lay in the field of conciliation of industrial disputes.[6] The Conciliation Act of 1900, the Railway Labour Disputes Act of 1903 and the Industrial Disputes Investigation Act of 1907 were three cautious but significant steps towards a federal role as umpire in labour disputes. Although much of the labour field fell under provincial jurisdiction, the department's services under the Conciliation Act were offered if both parties agreed, and with no compulsion on them to accept suggestions or findings. Of almost 700 disputes in Canada between 1901 and 1907, 41 were referred to federal conciliators, with 33 settlements resulting.

From these modest beginnings, and in response to some especially tempestuous times in railway labour relations in the early 1900s, the government moved a hesitant step further into

Within a short time after the discovery of massive silver deposits in Cobalt, Ontario, in 1903, the town became a thriving centre of activity. Here it is photographed as it appeared c. 1908. *Canadian Annual Review, 1908. Metropolitan Toronto Library Board.*

the bargaining process. Since 1898, the Trades and Labour Congress (TLC) had been toying with the concept of compulsory arbitration, but the federal government had cited provincial rights as reasons against taking it up. However, a draft government bill in 1902 included it to apply in railway disputes which had reached an impasse and which involved lines under federal jurisdiction. The chief purpose was probably to stimulate reactions from both labour and management with the expectation that they would be mostly negative, and this in fact happened. The Railway Labour Disputes Act was eventually passed and provided for compulsory *conciliation* by a tripartite board representing the parties and the public interest, followed by non-binding arbitration and public announcement of the resultant findings. In the eyes of the cautious King, the law's purpose was "to afford a means of the public getting an intelligent view of the facts of the situation and of bringing an enlightened public opinion to bear."[7] As William Mulock put it to the House of Commons, compulsory arbitration would have been "in advance of public opinion."

Four years later, this compulsory investigation approach was broadened in the Industrial Disputes Investigation Act which was to "aid in the prevention and settlement of strikes and lockouts in mines and industries connected with public utilities." It was probably the first such legislation anywhere with such broad application. A prolonged strike in the Alberta coal fields, principally concerning union recognition, had brought severe hardship to miners and public alike, and had convinced Mackenzie King that "a recognition of the obligations due society by the parties is something which the State is justified in compelling if the parties themselves are unwilling to concede it." The legislation provided that the government

Activities of the Mounted Police extended farther and farther north, thanks to mining and other developments, and to the necessity of protecting Canadian sovereign rights. This Royal North-West Mounted Police patrol set out from Dawson for Herschel Island in the last days of 1909.
Public Archives Canada, PA-29622.

could, on application from only one party to a dispute, set up a tripartite conciliation board, which might also go on to arbitrate the issues and publicize its findings. An important new aspect was that recourse to strike or lockout was prohibited prior to or during the period of reference to the board.

Organized labour's responses to the government's compulsory conciliation policy were mildly favourable to begin with. The TLC convention of 1907 passed a resolution of support, which more than outweighed the hostility of the radical Western Federation of Miners, which termed the Act "another instrument in the hands of the employing class for the subjugation of the working class." Yet, by 1911, even the TLC, largely composed of moderate unions of skilled craftsmen, was calling for repeal: in its view, the ban on strikes during time of reference to the board often was disadvantageous to workers. The argument was that they needed to choose their time of maximum pressure on an employer, especially when they were pretty sure he would not accept any arbitration recommendations which were even mildly pro-union or neutral. Yet the Act certainly did some useful service. In the 1907-1911 period there were 106 applications for conciliation (44 concerning mines or smelters, 58 in transportation or communications, and 3 in other industries where both parties had joined in the request). Most applications came from employees who must have been pleased that 90 per cent of the cases conciliated and/or arbitrated were settled without recourse to a strike.

But clearly the Act offered no real protection against powerful employers who were determined to avoid or emascu-

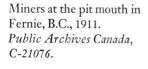

Miners at the pit mouth in Fernie, B.C., 1911.
Public Archives Canada,
C-21076.

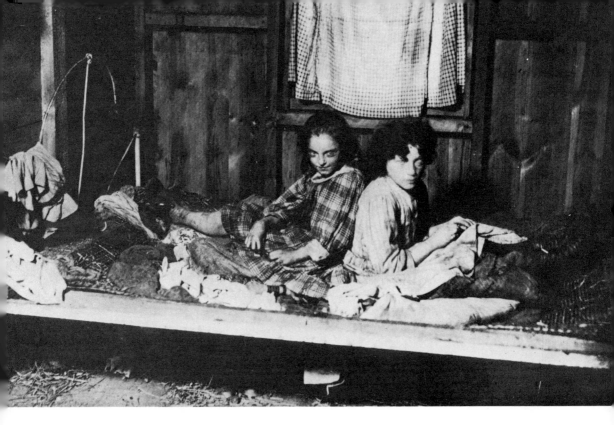

late unionization and who had a surplus labour market, often outside Canada if necessary, from which to recruit strike-breakers. In 1910 alone there were several instances of corporate power triumphant. In Sydney, Nova Scotia, coal miners, members of the United Mine Workers, surrendered unconditionally in April after a strike of over eight months, and without winning recognition of their union. With the help of Mackenzie King, an exceptionally bitter conflict between the mighty Grand Trunk Railway and its eight to nine thousand conductors, brakemen, switchmen and baggagemen seemed to have been settled. Later, however, it developed that a number of strikers were not re-hired, many more were denied their former job levels, and accrued pension rights were cancelled. King was accused, with some justification, of having been taken in by the GTR's American president, Charles Hays. For his part, King reported angrily to Laurier about the Hays-style attitude to labour:

> Railroading in the United States is a business which with a certain school of men is run on certain principles. One is that human life, to say nothing of human feelings, is not to be considered either as respects its loss through accident or its

Social problems were largely overlooked in the hectic prosperity of the Laurier era. This photograph, taken in Winnipeg in 1912, was entitled "The One-Room Home" and carried this caption, "The Shame of Large Cities. Eating, drinking, sleeping, working, playing, dying all in one room. It is time that every large city put an end to such diabolic conditions — what is your city doing about it?" Annual Report of the Superintendent of Neglected Children for the Province of Manitoba, 1912. *Public Archives Canada, C-30936.*

Salaries for sports stars in the days when a dollar was a dollar.
Ottawa Free Press, 1909. *Public Archives Canada, C-83827.*

massacre as a means to an end. The end is the power of money as against all other powers in the world. To admit the solidarity of labour in any industrial dispute is to admit something more powerful than money, and that must not be done, no matter how great or how tremendous the cost.[8]

The federal government's activities as a sort of umpire, or similar behaviour by the provinces, were no countervailing force at all to that sort of power and attitude.

One of the means by which employers maintained their advantage over trade unions in these years was that Canadian immigration and alien labour policies obligingly supplied them with a steady torrent of cheap non-unionized labour. The popular image then and since of the Laurier government's immigration policy was that it was aimed at the agricultural settlement of the prairies. So it was, but something in the neighbourhood of 70 per cent of the newcomers actually took work in industry or transportation. And this was not entirely by accident: active promotion of the importation of unskilled industrial immigrant labour was undertaken by a host of Canadian corporations and business associations, sometimes with the acquiescence of the federal government.

Electrical household appliances were still few and far between in Laurier's day, but in 1909 Eaton's offered this hand-operated "Chatham" vacuum cleaner. It was described as consisting of "a very powerful though very compact suction pump, a tank with dust trap on the interior, a good length of rubber hose, a brass tube and a peculiar flattened nozzle. The work is done by a lever that a ten year old child can push and pull for an hour at a time." The price was $25.00. *Archives, Eaton's of Canada Limited.*

The railway construction frenzy of these years put a particular premium on the provision of strong backs at cheap prices. Large numbers of sturdy workmen, generally referred to as navvies, were drawn from Britain, the Orient and central or southeastern Europe, much to the chagrin of Canadian organized labour.[9] British immigration was sizeable — almost a million came between 1901 and 1911 — but only a small proportion of it was unskilled labour of the kind the railways wanted. Too often for the liking of their employers, the British navvies with trade union backgrounds demanded organization rights and civilized working and living conditions in the construction camps. A disgusted Thomas Shaughnessy, the president of the CPR, wanted no more "men who come here expecting to get high wages, a feather bed and a bath tub." There were other sources, at least for a time. For years, Chinese coolies had been imported into the Pacific region; now, Japanese and Hindu labour was brought in too. However, it was not long before racially minded nationalists and job conscious workers put a virtual end to the practice, especially after savage riots in Vancouver in 1907. Between 1906 and 1908 the federal government made gentlemen's agreements with Japan and China to reduce the flow severely. Hindu immigrants were now required to bring $200 with them before being allowed entry. Attempts in 1909 by Charles Hays of the Grand Trunk to have the door opened up again were blocked by Laurier's judgment that "the peace of the province [British Columbia] would be really in danger" if he did.

That left the central and southeastern Europeans. Over half of the arrivals from that area during the Laurier years were in the unskilled labour category. Many went to work on the railways and in city construction. In 1904 alone, the arrival in Montreal of 3,000 Italians contributed to an unemployment total of between six and eight thousand Montrealers of that origin. Once construction on the Grand Trunk Pacific, National Transcontinental and Canadian Northern main lines was seriously under way after 1906, the flow became a flood. The railways begged the government not to interpose any barriers to it because the central and southern Europeans were "peculiarly suited for the work." Mackenzie King confided to his diary in 1911 that he and Frank Oliver, the Minister of the Interior, were opposed to this kind of immigration and favoured "making restrictions on virtually all save northern people of Europe." But, he lamented, the rest of the cabinet was determined to put having the railways built before quibbling about the nature of the immigrant labour force which did the job.

There was the same disinclination to interfere seriously in employment practices concerning the importation of non-immigrant alien labour from the United States, often brought in for strikebreaking purposes.[10] Federal legislation to regulate alien labour coming from the United States was put on the statute books in 1897 and it certainly was toughly worded, reflecting the general bitterness in Canadian-American relations at the time. The Canadian law was virtually a copy of a very stringent American one which was adversely affecting the

Laurier witnessed the birth of the automobile; the first passenger car in Canada was a Winton imported in 1898. In 1903 there were only 220 motor vehicles registered in Canada, and in 1910 passenger cars still numbered only 5,890. This photograph, taken about 1910, seems to record a meet of some kind. Left to right the cars are: a 1907 Russell (a make popular in Canada before the First World War); an electric coupe of a kind much favoured by well-to-do ladies of the day; a curious vehicle, with wagon-type wheels, produced for a time by the International Harvester Co.; and a recent model Reo truck. *Public Archives Canada, PA-38446.*

Flying began in the Laurier years. The Wrights flew late in 1903; in 1909 J. A. D. McCurdy, in the famous *Silver Dart* made the first flight by a Canadian in a heavier-than-air machine in Canada. Later that same year, he and his associate, Casey Baldwin, brought two planes (one of which is shown here) to Petawawa for trials which they hoped would impress the Canadian military authorities. But bad conditions ruined the trials and wrecked both their hopes and the *Silver Dart*. *Public Archives Canada, C-10999.*

employment of Canadians in border areas. Nevertheless, the TLC, by the time of its 1898 convention, condemned the Laurier law as "entirely unsatisfactory to the working people of this country." Enforcement was lax, as the government was loath to really anger the American government or Canadian employers. An amendment of 1901 went further, forbidding Canadian employers from advertising for labour in U.S. newspapers and outlawing completely the entry of non-American foreign workers through the U.S. Canadian labour spokesmen exulted, but found before the year was out that the CPR could still import hundreds of American strikebreakers without much trouble, because enforcement was left up to complainants, and few unions could afford the legal costs. Laurier appointed a Royal Commission to study the subject in 1904, and tougher legislation passed the House of Commons. But the Senate failed to agree and the Bill was not re-introduced subsequently during the Laurier administration, one reason being a court judgment that deportations under the Act would be illegal. As J. G. O'Donoghue of the TLC put it in 1909, the government's

policy was one of "shilly-shallying." The Minister of Labour, Mackenzie King, admitted as much in 1911, telling the House of Commons that imposition of alien labour penalties really depended on the interested parties. The nervous Canadian government did not appear to be one of them.

That organized labour was often in the van of anti-immigration efforts was hardly surprising. Frustrations about the impact of the surplus labour market on wage levels and unionization were only two of the reasons. An antipathy to the newcomers shared with the mass of middle-class Canadians was another. Racial stereotypes abounded. The *Hamilton Labour News* informed readers in 1902 that "Chinamen as citizens are not conducive to the best morals of a city ... The very smell of a Chinese laundry ought to be enough to send your clothes to a sanitary white man's laundry." The *Toronto Tribune*, a trade unionist publication, reacted in 1906 to the arrival of thousands of central and southern Europeans: "The commonest London loafer has more decency and instincts of citizenship than the Sicilian, Neapolitan, Croat or Magyar." The London *Industrial Banner* fulminated in 1908 that:

> The fellow who comes from Yurrup and makes talk with his hands has a cinch with the corporation ... If Canadians really want to get a chance today they should forget how to talk English, and practice up some kind of gibberish . . . Then they should let their hair grow on their face for a couple of weeks and do without washing.

S. R. Berry, a labour leader, protested in 1910 to Frank Oliver, the Minister of the Interior, against "the sudden influx of immigrants whose habits of life and moral characteristics are repugnant to Canadian ideals."

In Manitoba, Saskatchewan and Alberta the vast influx of non-Anglo-Saxon immigrants into hitherto lightly settled areas brought them into close contact with the Anglo-Saxon Canadians, Americans and Britishers who made up the rest of the population. As the size of the non-Anglo-Saxon group shot up after the turn of the century, concerns grew about the future cultural and ethnic character of the region.[11] The Saskatoon *Phoenix* commented in 1904 that a trip to the West could be viewed as a substitute for European travel. The Brandon *Times* reported that a group of newly-arrived "Galicians" — the term then applied to Slavs from regions of the Austro-

Hungarian and Russian empires in central and eastern Europe —
were "a sullen vicious looking lot" who seemed mostly to have
"considerably less than the average amount of intelligence."
Nevertheless, there were many who continued to prefer the
sort of view expressd by the Winnipeg *Tribune* at an early
stage in the influx, that the Galicians were a "strong and healthy
looking" work force to fill up the land and bring forth plentiful
harvests. In 1905, the Manitoba *Free Press*, seeing them at work
in all spheres of western life, pronounced: "They have initiative
as if by blood."

Initiative many of them certainly had; but there was much
questioning of the kind of style and way of life they were bringing to Canadian society. The Catholicism of most of the non-
Anglo-Saxon newcomers prompted widespread concern. To a
Dr. Hunter, writing in *The Presbyterian Record* in 1905, the
Galicians had been raised in an "ignorant, bigoted, superstitious
style of religion." The autocratic heritage of the churches of
southern, central and eastern Europe, he felt, was anything but
a healthy import. Protestant missionary work was pressed,
predictably without much result — both because of the lack of
religious and cultural commonality and because the French
Canadian-led Catholic hierarchy in the West determinedly
nourished the various transplanted national Catholic traditions.
For prelates such as Archbishop Langevin of St. Boniface, the
attempts to anglicize and Protestantize the Galicians, Poles and
others might also foreshadow the end of the cultural and religious distinctiveness of the frail francophone minority in the
West.

It was in the tax supported school systems of the West that
Canadianizing influences could be brought to bear most powerfully on the immigrant population. The Saskatchewan Department of Education promoted history as "the chief medium for
inculcating into the minds of our youths the facts and principles underlying the evolution of our Anglo-Saxon institutions." The "education of the immigrant," it asserted, "must
be and is one of the chief duties, if not the chief duty of many
of our schools." A prime requisite for this, it believed, was "the
common medium of English." The Manitoba Department of
Education took a similar line:

Incongruous elements have to be assimilated, have to be

welded into one harmonious whole, if Canada is to attain the position that we who belong here by right of birth and blood, claim for her. The chief instrument in this process of assimilation is the public school.

In fairness it must be acknowledged that there was pretty widespread agreement among school officials and inspectors that the non-Anglo-Saxon immigrant children did well in the classroom. As early as 1897 an inspector in southeastern Manitoba found the Galician pupils there "bright, intelligent and most anxious to acquire a knowledge of the English language." An Alberta inspector in 1907 noted that the "foreign" students he saw were "making rapid progress in their studies." He even thought they grasped arithmetic "more readily than the average Canadian or American child." A Saskatchewan inspector in 1911 commented that he "never saw better rural schools anywhere than some of the new ones among the Ruthenians [a successor term for the people previously described as 'Galicians']." Thus there seemed to be excellent grounds for belief that in the West of the future the second generation of the immigrant groups would be well educated, fitted for full participation in society's tasks and entitled to the enjoyment of its rewards.

But, in linguistic and cultural terms, doubts persisted about the effectiveness of Canadianization. Manitoba's bilingual

Field sports have been a feature of outings of all sorts since early days, and by the late nineteenth century, Canada had developed track stars of international standing. Here Tom Longboat, the Onondaga Indian athlete, is running behind Alfred Shrubb, the English champion whom he bested on several occasions. In 1906 Longboat won a race with a horse over a 12-mile course, and he competed in the 1912 Olympic Games.
Canada's Sports Hall of Fame. Public Archives Canada, PA-50318.

school regulations, and the practical difficulties which all the provinces had in securing competent teachers for out-of-the-way heavily non-Anglo-Saxon districts, often left foreign languages more effectively presented to the students than English. Saskatchewan, perhaps making the best of a bad situation, maintained a Training School for Teachers for Foreign Language Communities, with inferior accreditation qualifications – especially in knowledge of English – permitted. This probably was unavoidable if some of the immigrant schools were to be staffed at all, but it did contribute to a *de facto* difference in quality of schooling that undermined the assimilationist purposes of the province's official English-only educational system. And, as Westerners self-consciously sought to put their pioneer conditions behind them and move towards twentieth century standards, inferior brands of schooling became increasingly unacceptable to educationists and the public alike.

For a variety of reasons, a more intense Anglo-Saxon English-Canadian nationalist conformism was making itself felt throughout the nation. The reaction to the rise of non-Anglo-Saxon immigration to unprecedently high levels was one cause. Another lay in the francophone-anglophone conflicts over bilingual schooling in Ontario and Manitoba. A third reason, increasingly important from about 1909 onwards, was that major military confrontation between the British Empire and the autocratic German and Austro-Hungarian powers began to loom as a very near and threatening possibility.

It was in this sort of atmosphere that in 1911 the German Catholic Congress and the Polish Catholic Congress felt it necessary to strongly re-affirm their commitments to what the Poles called "the right to Catholic and national schools." As in Ontario, where the pressures among the English-speaking majority for a severe curbing of bilingual schools were moving rapidly towards a culmination in the hard line Regulation XVII of 1912, the Manitoba bilingual system's days were numbered. As the West's most popular and influential newspaper, the Manitoba *Free Press* remarked in 1910: "This is an English-speaking province and it is the duty of the government to see that every pupil of the public schools is given a sufficient education in English to equip him, in part at least, for the business of life." It denounced the "non-English schools masquerading as bilingual schools." In 1916 they would be swept away.

C. W. Jefferys is now remembered best for his expert and meticulous drawings of historical personages, scenes and events, but in Laurier's day he was one of those who was directing the interest of painters to Canadian subjects, especially the Canadian landscape. In 1907 he paid a first visit to the prairies, was fascinated by them, and set out to capture their wide expanses and subtle colouring on canvas. He undoubtedly influenced the painters who would later form the Group of Seven.
Western Sunlight, Lost Mountain Lake, by C. W. Jefferys, 1911. The National Gallery of Canada, Ottawa.

In 1911, the war era, with social divisions accentuated by inflation and profiteering and with distrust of enemy aliens, lay only a short distance down the road for Canadians. Already, social strains in labour-management relations and cultural tensions between French-speaking and English-speaking, Catholic and Protestant, native and immigrant Canadians were rising sharply. In Ottawa the government was still led by a man of "sunny ways," of optimism, of broad tolerance, of what in most essentials was a non-interventionist approach to the market place and its social costs, and to the working out of the cultural ramifications of a mostly wide-open immigration policy. The political ascendency of such a leader was bound to become much more difficult to sustain. Intervention in economic and social matters, and Anglo-Saxonism as a touchstone for policies in immigration, education, external relations and defence, would now attract an increasingly broad measure of support.

5
The Two Solitudes

Montreal harbour at the turn of the century. Several ships of the Allan Line, then the leading company in the trade between Canada and Britain, can be seen in the distance.

Montreal harbour at the turn of the century. Several ships of the Allan Line, then the leading company in the trade between Canada and Britain, can be seen in the distance.

It HAD NEVER been easy for French-speaking and English-speaking Canadians to share many of the same national aspirations. Even when they perhaps appeared to do so, as in 1867 and 1896, the resemblance of view was more a matter of pragmatic compromises than anything else. This had been a fact of life for Laurier from the beginning of his career, and it had strongly conditioned his thinking and policy on so-called nationalist issues. The stability of French-English relations, as well as the

Notman Photographic Archives, McCord Museum of McGill University.

Prime Minister's lease on power, depended on his avoidance or discouragement of the emergence of issues on which polarization might take place. Yet both the two main cultural communities were uneasy in these years of imperialism, race thinking and rapid economic change. Manipulation, obfuscation, even the delights of prosperity, could not deter them for long from indulging in the pursuit of divergent dreams, reinforcing mutual distrusts and fears. In such an environment, Laurier, the man of sunny ways, could only be the loser.

There is no single explanation for the rise of *nationalisme* in Quebec in the early 1900s, but the militarist imperialism which caused the Boer War crisis first brought clear signs of its existence. As noted, the strength of the young Henri Bourassa's protests at Laurier's sending of contingents to South Africa had been one of the pressures influencing the Prime Minister by 1902 to stand firm against political, military and naval co-ordination of the Empire. Their apparent reconciliation left the young M.P. for Labelle still a new and interesting voice to be listened to by Quebec opinion. His personal blending of the *Rouge* and *Castor* traditions — he was Louis Joseph Papineau's grandson but his education had been intensely Catholic, even ultramontane — made him an appealing figure. Around him, over the next decade, there formed a distinct and powerful *nationaliste* movement expressing the deepest concerns of much of Quebec's youthful aspiring elite in the face of what they regarded as grievous challenges to their society's *survivance*. From a host of new organizations devoted to *nationaliste* causes and through an aggressive journalism unshackled by the old party disciplines, the new spirit grew.

The creation in 1903 of La Ligue Nationaliste Canadienne in Montreal was one manifestation. There were only a handful of members, essentially young men of the urban non-business middle class — writers, journalists and lawyers — but they were to become very prominent in Quebec life in years to come. Bourassa was not among them, but his eloquence, idealism, outspokenness and concern about threats to the long-term interests of French Canadians had brought them together. Their program consisted of calls for Canadian autonomy within the Empire, respect for provincial prerogatives, protection of minority language and school rights and an energetic economic development policy of Canada for Canadians. Like Bourassa,

they were not separatists, but were intensely French Canadian. The public subsequently heard much from them, particularly in the weekly *Le Nationaliste*, which began publication in 1904 under the editorship of one of their number, the dynamic Olivar Asselin. He was 30, a *Québécois* whose family had migrated to New England where he had written for the Franco-American press, volunteered for war service against Spain in 1898 and soaked up the spirit of American reformist muckraking journalism. He brought to *nationaliste* causes modern anti-establishment materialist perspectives. With Bourassa, he would supply much of the intellectual content of the movement, especially in the social field.

A more traditionalist strain in the movement came from organizations such as the vigorous Association Catholique de la Jeunesse Canadienne-Française, founded in 1904. Its constitution referred to the "special mission" of the "French-Canadian race" in North America, which was "in a special fashion attached to the Catholic faith, which is one of the essential and

Marc-Aurèle Suzor-Coté, one of the best known of the Quebec painters and sculptors in the French-Canadian tradition, executed this bronze in 1907. *Le Trappeur*, which is 11½ inches high and 25 inches long, is but one example of the continuing development of French-Canadian visual art which paralleled and sometimes interacted with the development of English-Canadian artists during the Laurier era.
Le Trappeur, *by Marc Aurèle de Foy Suzor-Coté, 1907. Art Gallery of Ontario.*

149

specific elements." Canon Lionel Groulx, an enthusiastic participant in the group, would recall the spirit at the core of the A.C.J.C., the Ligue and other such organizations in these years:

> These young people wanted a country which could belong to them, and not to the outsider; in this country, they were determined to exercise full rights, to say goodbye to the humiliation of the second class citizen. They sought also a province which would be theirs and not the cheap prize of the tycoons of American finance. This province, their French state, land of their forefathers, they strove to build on a Christian basis. . . . This was because they had faith in their Catholicism.[1]

All these concerns and attitudes were to find plenty of scope in the years that followed. Some of the same idealism — minus the Catholicism, for the most part — had been present in Laurier's generation of *Rouges* almost a half century before. But now among the Laurier Liberals the fires of anti-corporate, anti-outsider idealism burned low; in Laurier himself they hardly even flickered.

The concern with Catholicism brought about in 1905 an important political stage in the movement and a notable impact on public opinion. Parliament was creating the new provinces of Alberta and Saskatchewan, and a major crisis developed in Ottawa over Laurier's measures for protection of their Catholic separate schools. His initial provisions would have guaranteed the fully separate rights allowed when the Northwest Territories had been set up in the 1870s. But a storm of protest from English-speaking Protestants, including many Liberal politicians and editors, quickly developed. Clifford Sifton's resignation from the cabinet, W. S. Fielding's threat to follow him and the open revolt of the Toronto *Globe* forced a new policy: guarantees would apply only to the much watered-down denominational privileges permitted by Territorial ordinances of 1901. The Liberal party was reunited in English Canada, but Quebec annoyance now flamed up. Bourassa, another *nationaliste* Liberal named Armand Lavergne, and five Quebec Conservatives vociferously opposed the amended clauses in the House of Commons. Not surprisingly, they lost their struggle there, but they now stood out before their co-religionists and fellow *Québécois* as the only uncompromising defenders of Catholic minority rights. As Bourassa told the House: "conciliation is never good, it is never possible, between two contrary principles, between truth and error, between justice and iniquity." Laurier conceded to a supporter: "our friend Bourassa has begun in Quebec a campaign which may well cause us some trouble."[2]

Over the next two years that campaign continued, and trouble did occur. In 1906 the Lord's Day Act was presented to Parliament, not merely to protect the "day of rest," but also to require its observance in the sober manner desired by Protestant puritans. This would have been a revolutionary change in the lifestyle of Catholic Quebec, where Sunday horse racing, drinking and other amusements abounded. Archbishop Bruchési of Montreal had given the hierarchy's prior approval, but it soon became clear that public opinion in Quebec supported the vigorous opposition of the handful of *nationalistes* and French-speaking Conservatives at Ottawa. Ten thousand people turned out to a protest rally on Montreal's Champ de Mars before Laurier agreed to a Senate amendment making application of the law dependent on provincial agreement. The following year's *cause célèbre*, bringing the *nationalistes* even more public attention, was the motion in the House of Commons by the young Armand Lavergne that French should be placed on a footing of equality with the English language in all public matters under federal jurisdiction. Some minor changes were hurriedly made, notably in the publications of the Intercolonial Railway and the Post Office.

Battles over religious, linguistic and cultural matters in Ottawa did not long remain the chief focus of *nationalistes* in these years. Indeed, *Le Nationaliste* was devoting by far the greatest bulk of its space to matters of purely Quebec concern, especially involving economic and social matters. Quebec was in the midst of incredibly rapid industrialization, based upon hydroelectric power, pulp and paper and secondary manufacturing for the vast Canadian market for which Montreal, with its favourable rail and water connections and its pools of capital, was the pre-eminent metropolis. By 1911, almost one-half of Quebec's population was urban, with only one-third involved in agriculture. Yet in this world of enterprise and entrepreneurs French Canadians played few leading roles. The great companies, banks and railways located in the province were almost

all owned, and their operations dominated by, "les Anglais" — English Canadians, Americans and Britishers. English was far and away the language of business, as a traveller from France remarked after seeing Montreal:

> Visitors may pass whole weeks here . . . without ever imagining for a moment that the town is French by a great majority of its inhabitants. English society affects unconsciousness of the fact, and bears itself exactly as though it had no French neighbours. They seem to regard Montreal as their property.[3]

So it was with the timber leaseholds and hydro sites in the province's hinterland.

Political control in the province had passed to the Liberals in 1897; a decade later they were solidly entrenched with the devastated Conservatives barely surviving at all. Lucrative directorships and campaign funding bound the governments at Quebec City and in many municipalities to the big interests, which were able to secure extraordinarily advantageous terms for their leases, taxes and franchises. It was a not unfamiliar process in North America, but in traditionally Catholic and largely French-speaking Quebec, recently so agrarian, there was little of a countervailing industrial reform tradition. The *nationalistes* sought to change all this. In 1907, Bourassa and Armand Lavergne left federal politics for the provincial sphere, soon to offer independent support to the reform-inclined Conservative opposition in the Legislative Assembly. Laurier sped Bourassa on his way with the wry remark: "I regret your departure. We need a man like you at Ottawa . . . though I should not want two."

The Liberal machine beat him in his first attempt to win a seat, but in the 1908 provincial election he personally defeated Premier Sir Lomer Gouin. Lavergne and twelve Conservatives were also elected, doubling the opposition's strength against the still mighty Liberal majority. When the Legislature convened, Bourassa and Lavergne were the most aggressive critics of the administration, decrying corruption and graft, condemning the sacrificing of agricultural colonization to the greed of the lumber companies, and demanding proper public bidding on hydro concessions. In *Le Nationaliste*, scandal charges against provincial ministers were numerous, causing one of them, L. A. Taschereau, to denounce the editors as "bandits." An aroused Olivar Asselin then descended from the press gallery to strike Taschereau, with 15 days in jail as his reward.

For the first time since the early 1890s, provincial politics in Quebec were no longer a one party affair, and some issues of real substance were being brought to public attention. Unquestionably, the organizational base of the Liberal Party and the power of the forces behind it remained strong. Nevertheless, Bourassa's championing of agricultural colonization had widened his appeal among the clergy, traditional devotees of this policy. And his uncompromising attacks on the probity of establishment politicians had caused his reputation to soar among students and the educated young. What was more, his sally into provincial politics had done a great deal to solidify the connection of *nationalisme* with Quebec's French-speaking Conservatives, something tentatively begun previously in the House of Commons during the Autonomy Bills, Lord's Day Act and language squabbles. For the *nationaliste* leaders to build a serious challenge to Liberal power on these gains at either the provincial or federal level required the appearance of an issue which would strongly engage the concern of broad popular opinion. As Laurier put it to a friend: "It is true that for the moment he [Bourassa] does not attack me. How long will that last? I am going to tell you right away. That will last until the first difficulty I shall have to solve. What has happened in the past will happen in the future."[4]

It was the development of the so-called Naval Issue which gave Bourassa and his friends their touchstone. Equally dangerous for Laurier's political fortunes was the dramatic revival of the hitherto flagging imperialist feeling among English Canadians in which debate over this question resulted. The news from Britain in March 1909 was of grievous danger for the whole Empire: Germany was said to be fast overtaking Britain in naval construction, especially in the crucial dreadnaught battleship class. An aroused press and a frenzied Conservative opposition at length forced the Liberal government in London to double its naval building rate. Eight new dreadnaughts would be built to give the Royal Navy 20 by the end of 1912. There were still alarmists aplenty who doubted that even this could keep Britain marginally ahead of the Kaiser's navy by that time. The effect of all this clamour was not long delayed in Canada. For the first time since the Boer War, press, politicians and public became obsessed with an Empire crisis. The issue this time was not, as it had been in 1899, whether Canadians should help out in some far-off colonial squabble; nor did it concern some debatable profit-and-loss trade matter, nor a constitutional theory. Canada's very security and her trade beyond North America were protected by the Pax Britannica on the seas; a hostile power in control of them would be a direct threat.

Accordingly, early Canadian reaction mostly reflected a sense of genuine concern and urgency. Predictably, most English-language Conservative newspapers and very many leaders in the business, civic, church and academic spheres were quick to urge a generous Canadian contribution towards the dread-naught building program. Even the normally non-imperialist and anti-militarist Liberal Toronto *Globe* urged Canada to "fling the smug maxims of commercial prudence to the winds and to do more than her share in the game of turning dreadnaughts from the stocks." In an anti-imperial vein, there were a few stirrings of alarm from a handful of Liberal news-papers, chiefly in Quebec and rural Ontario, and from some labour and farm organizations. Common to all were serious doubts about the magnitude of the actual crisis and fear lest the country be seduced by Europe's militaristic spirit.

Parliamentary debate on the issue took place almost imme-diately, on March 29 on a motion of George Foster, the Con-servative M.P. for North Toronto:

> In view of her great and varied resources, of her geographical position and national environment, and of that spirit of self-help and self-respect which alone befits a strong and growing people, Canada should no longer delay in assuming her proper share of the responsibility and financial burden incident to the suitable protection of her exposed coast-line and great sea ports.

Foster was fearful of the developing German naval threat and wanted to see Canada do her part to meet it. He opposed a fixed annual money contribution to the Royal Navy because "it bears the aspect of hiring somebody else to do what we our-selves ought to do." Instead, he favoured the gradual develop-ment of Canada's own naval capability; he wanted "to see some-thing grafted on the soil of Canada's nationhood." However, he believed that there might well be an immediate or near grave crisis with Germany, necessitating an emergency policy by Canada. Accordingly, he told Laurier that "if, after care-ful consideration" he recommended to Parliament "a means for meeting that emergency adequately, by the gift of dreadnaughts or the gift of money, this side of the House will stand beside him in thus vindicating Canada's honour and strengthening the Empire's defence."

As Laurier rose to respond he well knew that many Con-servatives in the House and outside it, and not a few Liberals, favoured direct contributions to the Royal Navy, not only as an emergency measure but as the only loyal and imperial permanent approach to naval development by Canada. But he also expected that a goodly number of his Quebec, rural Ontario and working class supporters would tend to recoil from that "vortex of European militarism" he himself long had railed against. For the pro-Empire Canadians he pulled out all his rhetorical stops, stating that "if the day should come when the supremacy of Britain on the high seas will be challenged, it will be the duty of all the daughters of the nation to close around the old mother land and make a rampart about her to ward off attack." But he added, taking a line that would be his until August 1914: "For my part I do not think the danger is imminent." His stand at past Imperial Conferences had been that Canadian defence provisions, military or naval, should not impinge upon Canada's autonomy. He admitted, however, that the country was now "altogether behind the times" in naval development and "should commence to establish the nucleus of a navy" because "it would be folly to sleep in a sense of the fullest security." He closed by offering a substitute resolution. It included a pledge of greater defence efforts, an affirmation that "under the present constitutional relations," the "payment of a direct contribution" to Britain would not do, and gave promises to "promote the organization of a Canadian naval service in co-operation with and in close relation to the imperial navy" as well as to make any sacrifice that was required to assist in "the maintenance of the integrity and honour of the Empire."

Robert Borden, the Conservative leader, also had to worry about possible divisions in his following. He was "entirely at one" with the Prime Minister that "the proper line" should be "a Canadian naval force of our own." But he insisted that there should be no specific prohibition of direct contributions to the Royal Navy and that the promise to set up a Canadian navy should be accompanied by "some word which would indicate an intention to act promptly." Then, echoing George Foster, he warned: "The day might come — I do not know that it will come — the day might come . . . when the only thing we could do in the absence of preparation in this country would be to make some kind of contribution."

Laurier was more or less prepared to agree with both of these suggestions: he inserted the word "speedy" into the promise concerning organization of a Canadian naval service;

ARMAND LAVERGNE

and, though he continued to object in principle to direct contributions, he was prepared to restrict express prohibition to contributions described as "regular and periodic." By implication, an "emergency" situation might call for special action. Thus amended, the resolutions were approved by the House without dissent. On the surface at least, compromise and non-partisanship were the order of the day. Skillfully, the Prime Minister and the Leader of the Opposition had moved to neutralize the naval issue, avoid partisanship and eschew politics of polarization in their diverse country.

But it was too much to expect that things could stay that way. Politics after all involve people; divisions of opinion were bound to come from the two parties, representing as they did

Armand Lavergne.
Archives nationales du Québec. Collection Initiale.

differing combinations, groups, interests, values and sensibilities, especially on Empire and defence questions. Then too, unrepresented in the House of Commons in 1909 was the growing *nationaliste* movement in Quebec, always highly suspicious of any scheme or involvement smacking at all of imperialism. Laurier, the man of conciliation, would have his work cut out for him.

In January 1910, he and his government unveiled the details of their naval policy. A Canadian delegation had seen Admiralty experts in Britain, had rejected any direct contribution to the Royal Navy, and had come home with cost estimates on some modest beginnings on a national volunteer naval service. There would be five cruisers and six destroyers, at a cost of 11 million dollars plus. The cabinet would have authority to place the force on active service, including service under the Royal Navy, but Parliament would have to sanction this within 15 days. The more pro-Empire of English-speaking Liberals were appealed to on grounds that a *national* naval service would be a fresh centre of strength for Britain in war emergencies. The *Québécois*, farmers' organizations, trade unions and pacifists were to understand that a Canadian force of small ships would be far less a contribution to the arms race than would have been the gift of giant dreadnaughts to the world's largest fleet. As Laurier put it to the House on February 3:

In the settlement of political problems it is very seldom that a solution can be reached on pure abstract principles. When a conclusion is arrived at, it is reached by taking into consideration several points of view and a common ground has to be found upon which the different shades of thought, the different prejudices and passions, and the different shades of public opinion can be united. That is true everywhere; it is truer in Canada, perhaps, than in any other portion of the earth.

The Governor General, Earl Grey, explained the circumstances and situation to an English friend: "The only form of contribution which Canada can make to the Empire is to lay the foundation of a Navy of her own." He added:

ANNEE—No. 1 MONTREAL, LUNDI, 10 JANVIER 1910 UN SOU LE NUMERO

NNEMENTS :
on Quotidienne :
-Unis $3.00
. . . . $6.00
n Hebdomadaire :
. . . . $1.00
on Postale $1.50

LE DEVOIR

Rédaction et Administration
71A RUE SAINT-JACQUES, MONTREAL.
TELEPHONE :
REDACTION : Main 7460.
ADMINISTRATION : Main 746

Directeur : HENRI BOURASSA.

FAIS CE QUE DOIS !

NT LE COMBAT

n'a pas besoin d'une longue présentation.
son but, on sait d'où il vient, où il va.
oduisons, dans une autre colonne, le programme d'ac-
, de la société dont le *DEVOIR* est la première oeu-

rogramme que le journal va faire connaître à la foule,
r la diffusion et le triomphe.
les principes et les idées s'incarnent dans les hom-
estent par les faits, nous prendrons les hommes et les
rps et nous les jugerons à la lumière de nos princi-

R appuiera les honnêtes gens et dénoncera les co-

* * *

olitique provinciale, nous combattons le gouvernement
e nous y trouvons toutes les tendances mauvaises que
faire disparaître de la vie publique: *la vénalité,
lâcheté, l'esprit de parti avilissant et étroit.*
yons l'opposition, parce que nous y trouvons les ten-
s: la probité, le courage, des principes fermes, une
de vues. Ces principes sont admirablement réunis
alité de son leader, M. Tellier.
e groupe ne suivrait plus les inspirations qui le gui-
, il nous trouverait sur sa route pour le combattre
nbattons les hommes au pouvoir.
a situation est moins claire.
artis s'enlisent dans le marasme où gisait la p
il y a quelques années.
la conquête ou de la conservation du pouv
l mobile.
ans, des questions vitales se sont imposée
taires fédéraux: la guerre d'Afrique
ation des nouvelles provinces et le droi
on du Grand-Tronc-Pacifique et le ré
migration étrangère et le peuplemen

e de conspiration les deux grou
fus pour donner à chacun de ces
, la justice, l'intérêt national
aux intrigues de partis ou, pis
viduels.
ème où nous entrons en scène,
a de la plus haute importance
mouvement impérialiste: la

ous à une répétition de la
sera-t-il la dupe des machin
tis?
retentissant de M. Monk,
tuation dangereuse et abr

e Jacques-Cartier peut êtr
attitude avec fermeté, log

* * *

le triomphe des idées su
e parti, il n'y a qu'un m
dans les classes dirigean
toutes ses formes: devoir
De là le titre de ce journa
sourire certains confrères.
devoir public est tellement
ment à beaucoup d'oreilles
outiques où, sous couleur
itant la badauderie du publi
la caisse des grandes comp
principes, idées et programm
effet, y créer une impression
nt et ces rires nous confirment
rgente et le nom bien choisi.
on ne s'effraie pas de l'austérité
iété, au contraire.
ous ne donnerons pas à nos lecte
trouve à foison dans les journaux
ages", comme les appelait, un jour
ous aurons une rédaction assez variée
agréable qu'utile.
oses — fond ou forme — nous n'avons
rait possible de plaire à tout le monde n
. Notre ambition se borne à chercher à
nous prêchons: le devoir de chaque jour.
s mériter la bienveillance, l'encouragement
gens d'esprit et de bien. Quant aux autres, n

HENRI BOURASSA.

Il n'y a pas de doute que ça ne soit joliment, habilement combiné.

C'est un grand homme que ce gros homme; c'est aussi un gros homme que ce grand homme!

Et c'est pourquoi on l'a vu, c'est pourquoi on l'a découvert, c'est pourquoi il faut, comme disait M. Mousseau, "ouvrir le parapluie des convenances."

Aussi M. Gouin s'est-il mis le doigt profondément dans l'orbite; c'était bien taillé, sans doute, mais il va falloir recoudre, et cela ne passera pas tout-à-fait comme il l'avait imaginé.

Monsieur le premier-ministre connaît bien mal ceux à qui
affaire. Que la Cour d'
ou ne soit pas con
poursuite des
che ou ne m
et toute l
te affa
jour

A NOS AMIS

Les lecteurs du "DEVOIR" sont tous ou presque tous nos amis.

Le "DEVOIR" n'épargnera, pour défendre les idées qui nous sont chères à tous, aucun effort, aucun sacrifice. Nous sommes également assurés de la bonne volonté et du dévouement de nos amis.

Ils peuvent nous aider de maintes façons: en s'abonnant d'abord, et en faisant abonner leurs amis; en nous

Nous sommes d'aussi bonne race...

On vient de distribuer aux journaux de la province de Québec le rapport du ministre des Travaux publics et celui de la Commission des Chemins de fer "pour l'exercice terminé le 31 mars 1908."

Le 31 mars 1908, vous avez bien lu et cela vous dit à quel point encore, grâce à notre apathie, grâce à des habitudes demi-séculaires—où nous ne cherchons point, pour
moment, à faire la part de la
volonté—l'on se moque
ttawa.
anglaise possède,
mois, ces do-
analyser,
ux ex-
an-

LA VIE QUEBECOISE

LES ELECTIONS MUNICIPALES

QUEBEC BOUGE.—GRANDEUR ET DECADENCE DE "SIR GEORGES GARNEAU". — LES AMBITIONS DE M. CHOQUETTE ET LES INTRIGUES DU PARENTISME.—LES SURPRISES POSSIBLES. — L'ATTITUDE DES NATIONALISTES.

I

LE PASSE

Les gens de Montréal disent volontiers que nous sommes une ville paisible; ils disent même: endormie. Erreur profonde: comme le bon Homier, quelquefois Québec sommeille, mais il ne dort jamais... que d'un oeil.

L'annonce d'élections prochaines crée
jours dans notre "bonne" ville,
période de fièvre intense.
i cette année plus que jamais, les
municipales causent-elles de
n. Qui sera maire? C'est ce
demande, depuis le sommet
mant jusqu'aux rives en-
rivière Saint-Charles.
uel, comme vous le sa-
bais du nom de GAR-
row). On croit,
qu'il sera rempla-
français.
la mairie ne jouit
pularité que
(ou Garneau),
intègre, parlant
connaissant les
pouvoir par le
grâce surtout
nalistes.
fondu aussi
ns de neige
n'ait des
ntas à côté
neau. Tou
uébec. La
bie d'a-
Garneau
qui l'a-
nt le dos
hampions
Ville, po-
vaient le
rvateur.
M. Gar-
Saint-
ire de ne
la foule
ses dé-
lant, pré-
ressé
ssait pour
tre par
artisans les
ressés, mais
e centenaire
affection pu
éleva pas la
un geste de
les fêtes de
tre transformées
la conquête au
e campagne de la
mpêcha, en partie,
gramme impérialiste
nt pour que le mai-
compris que ce
moment pour lui d'ac-
de la main des vain-

ue digression nous fait voir
ection pour M. Garneau est
ssibilité. Disons du reste qu'il
ge pas, ou, s'il y songe, c'est
eul et en cachette..

* * *

II

L'AVENIR

Pendant tout ce temps-là, les parentistes avaient perdu le pouvoir. Mais ils n'avaient pas perdu l'envie d'y retourner.

Tenteront-ils vraiment d'y retourner? Cela est dans l'ordre des choses possibles, même probables.

Ils exploitent en leur faveur l'impopularité du maire Gurnow. Seulement, ils n'ont pas de candidats à la mairie. Ils en cherchent un avec rage, avec passion, avec douleur. Quelquefois, ils en trouvent, mais ils se rendent vite compte que tous leurs colosses ont des pieds d'argile.

C'est ainsi qu'ils ont successivement mis de côté, comme battus d'avance, le chef suprême du parentisme à Québec, M. Alexandre Taschereau, et des seconds violons comme MM. Cyrille Delâge, Rodolphe Audette, Georges Tanguay, etc.

Ils semblent aujourd'hui avoir arrêté leurs vues sur M. James McCarthy, autrefois de la Frontenac Gaz. M. McCarthy acceptera-t-il? Et, s'il accepte, sera-t-il élu?

C'est un Irlandais catholique, parlant parfaitement le français, intelligent, joli garçon, et très riche. Trop riche même, puisqu'il vient de laisser sa compagnie de gaz se fondre dans le trust de M. Forget.

Comme le prix du gaz a, depuis, triplé, le service des tramways diminué; il faut tout l'aveuglement des parentistes pour chercher à faire la lutte avec un candidat à qui on reprochera sans doute toutes ces choses.

Mais, me direz-vous, espérant avoir la majorité du Conseil, pourquoi ont-ils tant de difficultés avec le maire?

III

LE PRESENT

Ah! c'est que le gros candidat à la mairie, et celui dont les parentistes ne veulent aucunement, c'est le sénateur Choquette.

Je n'ai pas besoin de faire le portrait de celui que l'on appelle ici... le bouillant Achille. Le sénateur est une tête... certes, c'est une tête où il y a beaucoup de cheveux. Tour à tour député, juge, sénateur, mouche du coche, Ane chargé de reliques, le séna-

Seulement, il y a dans l'ombre, u
Némésis qui le guette, sous les trai
grassouillets et troubles de Siméo
Napoléon Parent. Le Louis XI m
pal a naturellement ses acolytes. O
vie le Dain, que nous pourrions
trouver dans M. Ulric Barthe, et le
aides, Tros-Echelles et Petit-Andr
seraient en M. Philippe Paradis
Sam Desrochers, — deux de nos fig
res politiques les plus connues.
M. Parent a juré que Choquette
le serait pas. Choquette a juré qu
le serait.
Attendons la fin: elle sera curieus
cette querelle de famille libérale
pourrait bien nous apporter des su
prises, dont le parfum ne sentira p
le lis.
Ainsi, j'ai su qu'on forcerait peu
être M. Choquette à expliquer co
ment il se fait qu'une fois déjà, cand
dat à la mairie, il abandonna brusqu
ment et la bataille et le poste de d
recteur du "Soleil".
Si l'on fait cela, ce sera curieux, et
les informations manquent, ou
l'attaque mollit, je fournirai au "D
voir", et avant peu, des renseign
ments inédits, et d'un pittoresq
achevé.

IV

LA LUTTE

La lutte sera donc chaude: et ju
qu'ici les adversaires se valent. On d
cutera sans doute la question de
gare centrale du Transcontinental
des autres compagnies de chemin d
fer. C'est une des plus grandes ma
propretés qui se soient encore vu
dans notre histoire politique. J'y co
sacrerai sous peu un article de re
seignements et d'enseignements
serait trop long aujourd'hui et l'esp
ce me manque. En attendant, les a
versaires commencent à se mesurer
l'oeil. Ils ne valent guère mieux
une que les autres et les honnêtes ge
n'auront que peu l'occasion de vot
On dit que bon nombre d'échevins a
tuels ne se représenteront pas.

V

LES NATIONALISTES

La bataille n'est pas encore engag
mais elle apportera des surprises. L
nationalistes et les conservateurs tie
nent la balance du pouvoir. Toute
jeunesse de Québec, les jeunes gens
profession, les jeunes marchands, co
mis, ouvriers, étudiants, sont nation
listes. C'est une grande force qui, do
nant avec ensemble, emporte général
ment la position.
Entre "parentistes" et "choquet
tes" il n'y a aucun choix à faire, ma
les coeurs se soulèvent trop, l'indign
tion finira par triompher, et déjà u
troisième candidature se dessine à l'h
rizon.
On parle de l'échevin Fiset, comm
maire. C'est un fort candidat. Il a
rait pour lui nombre de libéraux q
ne peuvent avaler Choquette; il hab
te dans Saint-Sauveur — la partie q
commandera le plus grand vote —
aurait pour lui le vote ouvrier, l
"bleus" naturellement, et les nation
listes, qui estiment en M. Fiset u
grande intégrité, de la générosité
caractère et une grande connaissan
des besoins de notre ville.
Je le répète, sur toute la ligne no
pourrions bien avoir des surprises. Pa
mi ceux qui sont gros candidats a
jourd'hui, il y en a qui, déjà, par
passé, ont disparu au dernier m
ment.

* * *

On nous dit que notre ami Hua
hésite à se représenter. La vie pub
que pour lui en a été une de sacrific
et d'abnégation.
Sa carrière municipale est belle
féconde. Il fit fermer les buvettes
sept heures les samedis soirs: pour ce
il fut traqué, poursuivi avec haine p
les hôteliers et leurs consorts.
Huart a laissé dans la vie publiq
le meilleur de sa vie, son temps
son argent. Mais il s'est conquis l'a
miration et le respect de tous, l'affe
tion des honnêtes gens. Ce fut un ap
tre dans Saint-Roch et s'il laisse
Chambre municipale, nous le verro
sous peu, il faut l'espérer, apporter a
parlement de la province l'appui
son jugement clair et de son patr
tisme ardent.

JEAN RENAUD.

RE DUSSAULT-TURGEON

DEUXIEME ACTE DE LA COMEDIE

s du Port pour-
on : c'est la
jour. On cons-
procédure, le
ondé de nos ac-
ex-ministre des

réclame de M.
ille dollars de
s lots 582A et
-nord, illégale-
honorable Adé-
s ministre dans
omer Gouin.
tile de repasser
triste affaire,
os lecteurs; il
r qu'elle entre
ne phase nou-
résultats pro-
de cette pour-

trente décem-
ait pas encore
Dans tous les
ncore rapportée
, à l'heure ac-
n'a pas à com-

emandeurs sont
Marchand. Il
ette affaire la
t ne s'est pas
reur ordinaire,
C'est le bâton-
u'elle a requis
me qui fut l'a-
contre Four-

bec, — prétendent que cette poursuite n'est qu'un paravent destiné à couvrir le gouvernement.

Un chef, haut, très haut placé, du parti ministériel, dit souvent: "Le temps est un grand maître." M. Gouin a-t-il voulu s'inspirer de cette pensée? *Chi lo sa!*

Mais il est permis de supposer, malgré sa promesse sacrée de soumettre toute cette affaire à la Cour d'Appel, que M. Gouin n'a pas des envies torturantes de discuter sans délai, devant les Chambres, cette affaire et le rôle qu'y a joué son cabinet.

A la prochaine session, il pourra donc, avec son air le plus *plausible*, son ton le plus doucereux et son geste le plus paterne, demander l'ajournement de la discussion, sous prétexte que "l'affaire est devant les tribunaux de *celleux provinceux*."

Applaudissements frénétiques aux banquettes ministérielles, et voilà! le tour est joué....

C'est une année de gagnée; à l'autre session l'affaire est toujours devant les tribunaux, et l'on ne pourra dignement la discuter que *lorseux-queux* ils se seront prononcés.

Et ensuite?

Ensuite M. Turgeon sera shérif, M. Gouin aura mis sur ses épaules dodues le manteau d'hermine tou-

*qui
bien que
reaux. Mais
Nous n'habitons*
des régions de l'oppo
*disent M. Larue, mon
M. Rodolphe Lemieux?...
du luxe, et je proteste. — Monsieur l'Administrateur, vous êtes d'une extravagance, d'une prodigalité scandaleuses, et je vous dénoncerai à votre* Bureau de Direction!

...L'encrier, sans être de bronze ou d'argent, a bien dû coûter trente sous. C'est du luxe aussi, mais du luxe de bon aloi.

Mes yeux, charmés, vont de cet objet à la grosse bouteille d'encre qu'on vient de m'apporter. Une bouteille, une pleine bouteille. De quoi barbouiller tout un ministère. Attendez un peu, Monsieur Gouin, nous vous en ferons boire!

Cependant que je m'absorbe en ces douces pensées, M. l'Administrateur est arrivé à moi:

— Monsieur, m'a-t-il dit, faites de ceci l'emploi qu'il vous plaira; je n'ai rien à y voir. Je vous aurais toutefois beaucoup de gratitude si vous vouliez désormais éviter les libelles...

— Monsieur, ai-je répondu, allez plutôt prêcher la pudeur aux Langelier (1), la résignation aux échevins et la douceur aux panthères! Libelliste *je suis,* libelliste *je resterai. Je n'y puis rien, et vous pouvez d'avance en prendre votre parti. Une ère nouvelle va s'ouvrir pour les huissiers et les avocats, et vous seriez vous-même épouvanté si vous pouviez prévoir*

lent pratiquer aux flancs de la métropole les grandes saignées auxquelles ils se sont fait la main dans la banlieue, ou parce qu'ils n'ont ni "jobs" ni secours électoraux à attendre de la liste No 1, ou encore parce qu'ils brûlent eux-mêmes de l'envie des cinq mille piastres par année.

M. le sénateur Casgrain a pris part à la création du Comité civique où la liste No 1 a été adoptée *UNANIMEMENT*. Il était évidemment mécontent du choix, mais il n'a pas eu le courage d'enregistrer son dissentiment; cela donne une idée de la valeur morale de l'homme.

Le Nationaliste disait l'autre jour que, sous réserve de certaines garanties à exiger de tel ou tel candidat du Comité civique, la liste No 1 paraissait en somme fort convenable. C'est aussi l'opinion du *Devoir*, et le premier mot de notre journal au public canadien-français, touchant les élections municipales prochaines, est de se méfier des intérêts louches qui s'agitent derrière le prétendu mouvement populaire dont le congrès de ce soir est la première manifestation.

Les délégués du congrès ont été choisis par MM. Desaulniers, Treffé Bastien, Harris et autres, les

RDINAL SATOLLI

Le cardinal Satolli vient de succomber à la maladie qui le minait depuis des mois. Il était âgé de plus de soixante-dix ans.

Préfet de la Congrégation des Etudes, président de l'Académie pontificale romaine de Saint-Thomas d'Aquin, ancien délégué apostolique aux Etats-Unis, le cardinal Satolli aura été l'un des bons serviteurs de l'Eglise. C'était une intelligence distinguée, servie par de très fortes études.

Le cardinal Satolli s'est particulièrement intéressé au perfectionnement des études ecclésiastiques. On dit couramment qu'au dernier Conclave, c'est lui qui vainquit les suprêmes résistances du cardinal Sarto.

Nous lui devrions donc, dans une certaine mesure, l'accession au trône du pape actuel.

NOTRE CHRONIQUE FINANCIERE

Nous commencerons demain la chronique quotidienne des opérations de bourse à Montréal. Basée sur des renseignements fournis par les financiers les mieux réputés de la métropole, elle sera pour nos lecteurs d'un grand secours dans

LE "DEVOIR" AU DEHORS

NOS DEPOTS DE L'EXTERIEUR

Nous avons organisé, dans les principales villes un service de dépôts qui permettra à tous nos amis de se procurer le plus rapidement possible le *DEVOIR*.

C'est ainsi qu'à

OTTAWA

tous les soirs, vers les huit heures on trouvera le journal dans les dépôts suivants: 52, rue Rideau chez M. L. Sarrazin; 254, rue Dalhousie, chez M. A. Beauchamp; 239, rue Rideau, chez M. Desjardins; 280, rue Dalhousie, chez M. L. Guldbrandsen.

Le même soir, également, on trouvera le *DEVOIR* chez M. J. B. Fontaine, à Joliette; chez M. Lucien Addison, à Lachine; chez M. J.-A. Rabeau, à Lachine Locks; chez M. Lorenzo Perras, à Longueuil; chez M. Armand Brousseau, à Saint-Hyacinthe; chez M. Onésime Duval et dans sept ou huit autres dépôts de Trois-Rivières: chez MM. R. Mailhiot et C

> Many Ontario men are prepared to give dreadnaughts and liberal money contributions, but the province of Quebec is opposed to anything of this sort. The French Canadians will however support a Navy which is constructed, owned, manned and controlled by Canada.[5]

His words would prove accurate about "many Ontario men," and other English Canadians, but turned out to be rather over-optimistic concerning the French Canadians. To some extent he was confusing Canada with the Liberal Party.

It was the Conservative Party, with its electoral strength predominantly outside Quebec, which was most open to strong imperialist pro-contributions pressure. Shortly after the passage of the 1909 resolution by the House of Commons, Premier Sir James Whitney of Ontario publicly regretted that eight or ten million dollars had not been appropriated for dreadnaughts. Another Conservative Premier, Roblin of Manitoba, announced that people in his province were unanimously and enthusiastically in favour of such a course, and he denounced the "toy navy" intended by the Laurier government. Premiers McBride of British Columbia and Hazen of New Brunswick took similar lines, as did the Party's leaders in Saskatchewan and Alberta. "Dreadnaughts, not talk," was the Toronto *Mail and Empire*'s demand, and it was joined by most of the Party's other English-language newspapers. No doubt political opportunism played a part in this, but a sincere sense of Canada's duty to an Empire perhaps about to be gravely imperilled seems to have been a significant factor too.

For some time, Borden kept very largely to the lines of the resolution of March 1909 although he reminded Party members in favour of a dreadnaught gift that an emergency contribution was not, thanks to him, ruled out. Whether or not an emergency actually existed was known only to the British and Canadian governments, and he awaited clarification from them before coming to conclusions.

Borden's position was doubly difficult because the French-speaking Conservatives of Quebec, led by Frederick Monk, and in close collaboration with their provincial allies, Bourassa's *nationalistes*, had moved to attack *any* naval expenditure by Canada. The Quebec Conservative paper, *L'Evénement*, warned that a Canadian navy would drag the country into all of Britain's wars, whatever the issues involved. Montreal's

Le Nationaliste claimed the government had "sold out to England." On November 8, 1909, Monk openly denounced the March resolution. Canada, he insisted, should concentrate on building up her own resources. She had no obligation to defend other parts of the Empire or Britain's naval supremacy. Any other attitude, he believed, would destroy Canada's self-government, and it would be manifestly unjust to settle such a question finally without submitting it to the judgment of the electorate. When Henri Bourassa's new daily, *Le Devoir*, commenced publication in January 1910, it announced that Monk "can be assured of our support, if he maintains his attitude with firmness, logic and perseverance." With the confirmation of the details of Laurier's naval policy in 1910, the first substantial challenge to his federal power in Quebec for 14 years appeared to be inevitable at the earlist available electoral opportunity.

Borden, in responding to Laurier's Naval Service Bill of 1910, was initially cautious and conciliatory during debate on first reading. Not a militarist, he stressed however Canada's debt to the Empire and her need of sensible preparedness in a stern unfriendly world. He told the House: "Take the facts and nothing but the facts as they are known today, and no one can dispute that the naval supremacy of Great Britain . . . is openly and avowedly challenged." He begged the Prime Minister, while going on "slowly, cautiously and surely" with his Canadian navy proposals, and giving the people "if necessary opportunity to be heard," not to forget the existence of "an emergency which may rend this Empire asunder before the proposed service is worthy of the name." But the advice was not taken, and on February 3, on second reading, he lowered the boom. The government's scheme, he argued, while very expensive, "will give no immediate or effective aid to the Empire and no adequate or satisfactory results to Canada." Veering for a moment towards Monk and the *nationalistes*, he opposed any permanent policy "until it has been submitted to the people and has received their approval." He concluded that "in the meantime the immediate duty of Canada and the impending necessities of the Empire can best be discharged and met by placing without delay at the disposal of the imperial authorities as a free and loyal contribution from the people of Canada" the funds for construction of two dreadnaughts.

In English Canada, Laurier's Naval Service Act, which

the Liberal majority in Parliament dutifully put through, did not become the key issue in the ensuing general election. As will be seen, the imperialist reactions to Laurier's approach on the naval issue were subsumed or replaced by the more powerful critical reactions to his reciprocity agreement of 1911 with the United States. But feelings were stirred up again in 1909-

1910 among many English Canadians that Laurier and the French-Canadian Liberals were "not British enough" when it came to a crucial question of Empire defence, and this constituted a major weakening of Laurier's political strength in the country. There were also some signs in these years of a renewal of the ethnic and sectarian antipathies over language,

The Eucharistic Congress parade, Montreal, 1910. *Public Archives Canada, PA-23772.*

separate school rights and the role of the Catholic Church in society, and these signs boded ill for the prolongation of a French-speaking Catholic's hold on federal power. The Ontario bilingual schools controversy was under way as a response, of both the Irish Catholics and English-speaking Protestants in the province, to French as a school language in the northern and eastern districts where substantial immigration from Quebec had taken place. And militant Roman Catholicism, as manifested by a Quebec court decision early in 1911 giving civil recognition to the Vatican's *Ne Temere* decree against mixed marriages, as well as in the huge Eucharistic Congress of delegates from all over the world, held in Montreal in 1910, tended to raise Protestant hackles. A leading Conservative organizer in Ontario wrote Borden some months before the 1911 election that he found "a strong prejudice against Sir Wilfrid on the 'mixed marriage' question and this with the Liberals. If the feeling in my county is any omen as to Ontario as a whole I believe we will surprise them."[6]

If the precise proportions of the anti-Laurier, anti-Quebec ramifications of the naval question in Ontario are difficult to discern, the same cannot be said of the anti-Laurier, anti-Liberal anti-imperialist reactions in Quebec. There the storm clouds thickened ominously throughout 1910. By the end of the year, the Governor General noted fear among Laurier's friends of a possible disaster at the hands of "Mr. Monk, Messrs. Bourassa and Lavergne and the Curés."[7] Day by day Henri Bourassa was mining a rich lode of isolationism and anti-militarism in *Le Devoir* and, regularly, before mammoth public meetings, his fiery oratory and intense emotion at last were striking sparks from more than just the young would-be elite. With Monk and other Quebec Conservative leaders on the platform with him at St. Eustache, scene of one of the *Patriotes'* defeats in 1837, Bourassa told an audience of 8,000 that Laurier had betrayed French Canadians by giving birth to a navy which would carry their sons to death in foreign wars of no concern to Canada, and by allowing the Catholics in many provinces to be prevented from having their children educated in their own language and religion. He added, with the crowd roaring its agreement:

I say that when a man, whatever his personal qualities may

This 1911 poster advertised for "strong, healthy and well educated men and boys" to join the newly created Canadian Navy. *Canadian War Museum, National Museum of Man, National Museums Canada.*

be, when a man scorns at such a time the confidence and love a people have placed in him, in order to betray with one blow all his own people, I say that a man like that is more dangerous for his faith, for his country, and even for the British Crown, than the worst of Orangemen.

When the crowd voted its virtually unanimous approval of a series of condemnatory resolutions, drawn up by Bourassa and agreed to by Monk, Bourassa almost wept as he said to them: "I thank you in behalf of your people, your country, your fathers, and above all your sons."[8]

The feeling gathering around him was intensely Catholic as well as *Québécois*. At the Eucharistic Congress in Montreal in September 1910, it was Bourassa who thrilled a crowd of thousands in Notre Dame Cathedral with an extemporaneous rebuttal of a suggestion by a prelate from Britain that English should be stressed as the language of Catholicism in Canada in order to keep or build up the Faith's strength with the vast new immigrant populations being grafted onto English Canada. "I do not wish, through a narrow nationalism to say . . . that the Catholic Church ought to be French in Canada," Bourassa remarked, but added:

> No, but say with me that among three million Catholics, descendants of the first apostles of Christianity in America, the best safeguard of the Faith is the conservation of the idiom in which during three hundred years they have adored Christ.
>
> Yes, when Christ was attacked by the Iroquois, when Christ was denied by all the world, we confessed Him and confessed Him in our language . . .
>
> Let one beware, let one be carefully aware, of extinguishing this fire, with its intense light which has illuminated a whole continent for three centuries . . .
>
> But, it is said, you are only a handful; you are fatally destined to disappear; why persevere in the struggle? We are only a handful, it is true; but in the school of Christ I did not learn to estimate right and moral forces by numbers and wealth. We are only a handful; but we count for what we are; and we have the right to live.[9]

The tumult in Notre Dame that day, the crescendo of cheers for him on the morrow as he walked through the city in the Congress parade — these were signs of the hero worship which Bourassa now was drawing from a wide public which was delighted with his outspokenness regarding their deep pride in their Catholicism and in their language, and their grave fear of assimilation and of death in foreign wars. For so many of them Laurier the conciliator, Laurier the fixer, Laurier the pragmatist would no longer do.

Laurier the politician fought back on several fronts. He sent emissaries to bishops and even to the Vatican to counter the work of prelates, clerics and religious publications whose hostility to his naval and other policies was increasingly outspoken.[10] And he lashed out publicly against his critics and tormentors at a Party rally in mid-October, denouncing those who seemed to want a purely French party and to clothe it in purely Catholic garb:

> This violent section — you know it — comprises the Pharisee end of Canadian Catholicism; those who have constituted themselves the defenders of a religion which no one attacked;

those who handled the holy-water sprinkler as though it were a club; those who have arrogated to themselves the monopoly of orthodoxy; those who excommunicate right and left all whose stature is a little greater than theirs.

Laurier then challenged the *nationaliste*-Conservative alliance head-on. He opened the seat of Drummond-Arthabaska for a by-election to take place on November 3. Supposedly, it was a safe Liberal seat. It had been in the Party's hands since 1887; in addition, the Prime Minister had practised law in Arthabaska and still maintained a summer home there. "The *nationalistes* want to fight us," declared the Liberal candidate, J. E. Perrault, "let them come on then." The challenge was taken up, with Bourassa, Lavergne and Monk invading the riding to meet a battery of federal cabinet ministers. The *nationaliste* candidate was Arthur Gilbert, a young local farmer. His slogan was: "A vote for Perrault is a vote for war; a vote for Gilbert is a vote for peace." Bourassa charged: "A day will come when draft officers will be scouring the country and compelling young men to enlist either in the navy or in the army, to go to foreign lands and fight the battles of Great Britain." There was a tide running, and on November 3 the previous Liberal majority of 834 became a *nationaliste* one of 207.

In vain Laurier denounced the "demagogues" who had beaten his candidate, and claimed that some defeats were more honourable than victory. But even his own oratory, the power of patronage and the legendary organizing skill of the Liberal Party in Quebec could not turn the tide by the time of the general election in September 1911. Laurier still took 38 of the 65 seats, but this represented a net loss of 16. The Quebec bloc, his traditional power base, was weakened, with *nationaliste* fervour and oratory an effective complement to the normal Conservative note. An "unholy" alliance it might be but to pragmatic Conservative organizers both inside and outside Quebec, any successful assault on Laurier's strength was cause for applause. The 1911 election saw two quite separate campaigns — one in French-speaking Quebec, and another one, quite distinct, everywhere else. But Laurier was obliged to stand for more or less the same things in both of the "two solitudes." By 1911 the country was so much at odds with itself that this position had become immensely difficult.

6
Pride and Power

WE WELCOME CANADA'S GREATEST SON TO CANADA'S NEWEST CITY

ONCE IN A LONG WHILE a democracy may experience an election campaign dominated by a single great issue, illuminating deep emotions and power relationships. In Canada in 1911 there was such an issue — the Laurier administration's proposed reciprocal trade agreement with the United States. Of course there were other important features of that campaign, particularly the clash in Quebec over the naval question between Laurier and the *nationaliste*-Conservative "unholy alliance," but the reciprocity debate overshadowed them all, and was decisive, ending the Laurier era.

Political change in Ontario was central to the electoral overturn, but the seeds of the process were sown elsewhere. One locus was in the West. Throughout the frenzied years of wheat boom, railway building and mass immigration the West had been maturing, but not as a fully contented adjunct of older Canada. For increasing numbers of its inhabitants there was annoyance concerning their dependence on the whim and fancy of the big interests back east. The elevator companies, the railways, the banks, the retail houses, the manufacturers of Montreal, Toronto and other nefarious mercenary cities had very real power over their lives. By 1905, many farmers, to quote a Winnipeg grain buyer, had decided that "all grain buyers are thieves, and hell's divided equally between the railways and the milling companies."[1] The National Policy tariff wall and the freight rate schedules never ceased in the Laurier years to prompt these frontier complaints of victimization, so familiar for generations in North America.

But while the good market prices after the mid-1890s continued in Britain and Europe, while farm and equipment mortgages were cheap, and while spectacular settlement went forward, the grumbles in the West did not add up to anything like a crisis. The government in Ottawa, after all, was the same one which had settled so many westerners on the land, and so cheaply. The man who had presided over that great success story had been a westerner, Clifford Sifton of Manitoba; and his successor in 1905 as Minister of the Interior was an Albertan, Frank Oliver. The new provinces of Alberta and Saskatchewan were loyally Liberal from the outset, and Liberals in all three prairie provinces could anticipate having increasing influence within their national party, seemingly unbeatable at the polls.

OPPOSITE
The welcoming arch erected in Prince Rupert to greet Laurier when he was making his famous western tour in 1910. The city was incorporated the year of his visit.
Public Archives Canada, PA-95618.

169

Yet there were disquieting signs as the first decade of the new century drew to a close, that national policy, in regard to the tariff, was being confirmed in essentially protectionist patterns. In the revisions of 1907 a new intermediate tariff was inserted between the high protectionist rates and the lower British preference on goods from countries prepared to make reciprocal concessions to Canada. Whatever freeing of trade this might achieve with European countries, the barrier to cheaper exchange with the protectionist U.S.A. remained very high: it seemed that there would be no real interference with the manufacturers' tariff.

Westerners and farmers generally were organizing in these years to further their interests, while economic circumstances were becoming less agreeable. Co-operatives, such as the Grain Growers' Grain Company in Manitoba and farmer-owned elevator systems in Saskatchewan and Alberta, were giving agricultural producers greater clout in the marketplace. In 1907 the three prairie farmer groupings, the Manitoba Grain Growers' Association, the Saskatchewan Grain Growers' Association, and the United Farmers of Alberta, joined together in a common council; and the next year under their sponsorship, the *Grain Growers' Guide*, a sparkling, informative and highly political weekly, was launched. Alliance with the Ontario based Dominion Grange in 1909 produced at long last a potentially powerful national farm organization, the Canadian Council of Agriculture. Meanwhile, world grain prices began to fall in 1909, land values stood still or declined in the West and the farmers' familiar burdens of indebtedness became heavier. Conditions improved temporarily as the boom was not really over. But, less than ever was its continuance to be taken for granted. Farmer spokesmen — in the new organizations, in the press and in the old political parties — pressed anew their claims for public policy more to their liking, less in line with what they saw as the dominance of the big interests, mostly eastern.

Such was the situation in April 1910 when Sir Wilfrid Laurier announced that he would make an extensive summer tour throughout the West. He had not done so since 1894, and his aging administration, unable to please both Quebec and Ontario on the naval issue, and none too impressive administratively after 14 years in office, needed to find some new

well-spring of energy. The year before, the Prime Minister had consoled a defeated Liberal candidate: "What has happened to you in your county will happen to me before long in Canada. Let us submit with good grace to the inevitable."[2] The philosopher, now on the verge of 70, could write the words, but the combative politician, actor and lover of power could not permit his career to just peter out. As his train steamed west from Ottawa in the late June sunshine the youthful old man with the eye-catching plume of white hair, always faultlessly dressed in the style of bygone years, dreamed of his prospects, not his past. There were currently 27 seats representing the three prairie provinces, in a House of Commons of 221. He had taken 15 of them in 1908, having trouble only in Conservative-dominated Manitoba, with its high proportion of British and Ontario stock. A new census would be taken in 1911, with a major redistribution of House seats in the prairies' favour a certainty. Liberalism might reign a long while yet, perhaps well past its old chieftain's time, if he could link it firmly with the aspirations of this potentially pivotal region.

By the time the tour ended, at Winnipeg on September 3, he had a pretty clear idea of what those aspirations were. At every stop, from almost every person he met, the loudest pleas by far were for lower tariff duties. The Manitoba Grain Growers' Association was characteristically blunt:

> Of the many economic questions which engage the attention of western farmers, none is regarded with so much disapproval as the protective tariff. Nor is there any feature of the policy of the federal government that has been so burdensome to the western farmers, or has been the means of retarding the development of the country and hampering the progress of the early settlers as has the element of protection that obtains in the customs tariff of Canada.

They even had the cheek to remark that they could not better express the western farmers' viewpoint than by quoting from the Liberal Party's platform of 1893 the promise to change the tariff "as to make free or bear as lightly as possible upon the necessities of life" and "to promote freer trade with the whole world, more particularly with Great Britain and the United States." Particular concern was expressed that duties be lowered on agricultural implements, cement and woollen goods. Laurier good-naturedly explained that it had been the Americans who for years had blocked progress in reciprocal tariff reductions. "So I have said, 'Good-bye, Washington; we will make no more pilgrimages. We will be independent, and try to build up trade for ourselves' — and the next pilgrimage came from Washington to Ottawa."

That "next pilgrimage" he was referring to was a recent development in the astonishing new friendly American trade diplomacy towards Canada, then unfolding. Though quite possibly a passing phase, the Taft administration's evident interest in exploring mutually advantageous tariff reductions provided the Prime Minister with a welcome opportunity to find ways to cater to this outpouring of prairie opinion. When Laurier's 57 major meetings and the countless whistlestops ended at last on September 3, and he headed wearily home to Ottawa, he was no doubt impatient to see what would happen when formal trade talks opened with the Americans in Ottawa in two months' time.

The new American friendliness sprang almost entirely from political pragmatism. For years, the high-tariff wing of the Republican Party had been in the ascendent in Washington. Even in 1909 it had possessed enough power to dictate the terms of the Payne-Aldrich tariff legislation, by which special maximum duties, 25 per cent higher than the general ones, would fall on imports from any country that "unduly discriminates against the United States or the products thereof." Canada's three-tier tariff of 1907, and a Franco-Canadian trade pact under it in 1909, giving France the intermediate rate on some exports, made the application of the Payne-Aldrich tariff to Canada seemingly inescapable. This was distressing news to American consumers of Canadian natural resources, especially the newspaper publishers who were dependent on Canadian pulp and paper; and, it threatened to bring on a revolt by the increasingly significant low-tariff "progressive" wing of the Republican Party. President William Howard Taft, eager to mollify both elements, pressed Canada to apply her intermediate rates to a very small select list of minor items in American trade on which France was already benefitting from lower charges. Agreement was reached in March 1910, and the President exempted Canada from Payne-Aldrich penalties. He also sent an unprecedented "message to the people of Canada," through Laurier's representative, that it was his "deliberate purpose to promote in such ways as are open to me, better trade relations between the United States and Canada than at present exist." Scant days later, an official American request for negotiations on broader and liberal trade accords went to Ottawa. It was a far cry from the American mood of Alaska award times or the anti-Canadian atmosphere which had accompanied the enactment of the McKinley and Dingley tariffs in the 1890s. It would have been undiplomatic in the extreme for Laurier to have declined to enter these negotiations, especially since, on a broad range of other issues, Canadian-American and Anglo-American relations had become so amicable in the last few years. Intensive co-operation among Laurier, Governor General Lord Grey, the British Ambassador in Washington, James Bryce, and the American Secretary of State, John Hay, on fisheries, boundary issues and other contentious questions had brought about several significant agreements, most notably the Boundary Waters Treaty of 1909, establishing the International Joint Commission.

The negotiations opened in Ottawa on November 4, 1910. A week of manoeuvring showed the Americans that a treaty covering a truly comprehensive list of manufactured products was out of the question: manufacturer pressure on the Canadian cabinet was too strong. The president of the Canadian Manufacturers' Association had declared in November that the country neither needed nor wanted reciprocity, except perhaps in a "limited number of natural products." Yet a giant farmers' "siege of Ottawa" in December, while the negotiations were in recess, powerfully renewed the reverse pressure. Politically, the Laurier government would have to square the circle. When the talks with the Americans resumed in Washington in January 1911, it was soon clear that the Americans were so anxious to reach agreement that Canada was virtually able to write the terms.

These were reported to the House of Commons on January 26 by an ebullient W. S. Fielding, the Minister of Finance, to the delight of Liberal M.P.'s and to the dismay and discomfiture of Conservatives. Initial reaction in the House and the press was that the government had scored an incredible coup. Borden recorded "the deepest dejection" among Tories. There would be reciprocal free trade in farm animals, grain,

Discouraging the intimacy between Miss Canada and John Bull

fruit and vegetables, dairy products, fish, salt, and rough lumber; lowered duties on some food products, agricultural implements and building materials; and reductions on a very small list of manufactured articles, including plumbing fixtures, clocks and engines. To avoid the necessity of gaining the U.S. Senate's two-thirds' approval of treaties, implementation would be by concurrent legislation. As if by magic – but actually mainly as a result of American political exigencies – the Canadian government was moving to meet the main demands of the prairie farmers, while leaving the protective tariff on manufactures virtually untouched. The Conservative Ottawa *Journal*'s initial reaction was not untypical: it called the agreement "a staggering surprise" and "an excellent thing . . . for this country." On that same side of politics, the usually aggressive Toronto *News* had to concede that the provisions were "difficult for Canada to reject." The western farmers, naturally enough, were ecstatic: when the terms were wired to a meeting of the Manitoba Grain Growers, delegates stood and cheered wildly. With one stroke, it seemed, the Laurier ministry had been renewed and revived.

Yet, as the Canadian correspondent of the London *Times* reported to his readers, within 24 hours of Fielding's speech

One of the many cartoons inspired by the reciprocity controversy of 1911. *Courtesy of the Public Archives of Nova Scotia.*

there was "an undercurrent of unrest and dissatisfaction in financial and business circles." The undercurrent very soon became a flood, in the greatest spectacle of pressure group formation and activity in Canadian history. The protection of vested interests as well as the promotion of imperial and national ideals became involved. Actions of the at first profoundly shaken Conservative Parliamentary Opposition were initially less important in this process than were spectacular public demonstrations of anti-reciprocity sentiment by leading businessmen, important numbers of them hitherto identified as Liberals. Perhaps the single most significant incident occurred on February 20 when 18 prominent Toronto Liberals, leaders in business and finance, denounced the agreement. They included Z. A. Lash, solicitor for the Canadian Northern Railway; Sir Edmund Walker, President of the Canadian Bank of Commerce; J. C. Eaton, President of the T. Eaton Co.; R. J. Christie of Christie, Brown and Co., the milling and biscuit concern; G. A. Somerville, Managing Director of the Manufacturers Life; and W. D. Matthews, Vice-President of the Dominion Bank and a director of the Canadian Pacific. Other signatories came from a selection of banks, insurance companies and trust firms. They hailed Canada's "present unexampled prosperity" as the result of "the expenditure of hundreds of millions of dollars upon railways, canals, steamships and other means of transport between East and West and West and East." They argued that the reciprocity accord "would check the growth and development of trade between the various parts of Canada with each other, or between Canada and the various parts of the Empire." The conclusion went far beyond economics:

> Believing as we do that Canadian nationality is now threatened with a more serious blow than any it has heretofore met with and that all Canadians who place the interests of Canada before those of any party or section or individuals therein should at this crisis state their views openly and fearlessly, we, who have hitherto supported the Liberal Party in Canada, subscribe to this statement.[3]

Almost as grievous a blow to the government's position occurred eight days later when Clifford Sifton, Laurier's former right-hand man from the West, deserted his Liberal

Robert Laird Borden.
Public Archives Canada,
C-17946.

colleagues on this issue. Before packed public galleries and a tumultuous House, Sifton tore into the agreement: it would kill Canadian meatpacking and milling; it would bankrupt the railways; it would halt the flow of American capital into job intensive Canadian industries; and it would replace Winnipeg by Chicago as entrepôt and banker for the Canadian West. "These resolutions in my judgment," he thundered, "spell retrogression, commercial subordination, the destruction of our national ideals, and displacement from our proud position as the rising hope of the British Empire."

Meanwhile, almost every passing day was bringing new denunciations from organizations and interests wedded to the National Policy. The Montreal Board of Trade, the Dominion Millers Association, delegations to Ottawa of meatpackers and fruit growers in Ontario, the Winnipeg Grain Exchange and countless others went on record. The Toronto Board of Trade pronounced 302 to 13 against the agreement. The former president of the CPR, Sir William Van Horne, emerged from retirement to, as he put it, "bust the damned thing." He wrote a friend that, with reciprocity, Canada was "making a bed to lie in and die in."[4] Powerful propagandist organizations came into being: the Canadian National League in Toronto and the Anti-Reciprocity League in Montreal. As Governor General Lord Grey advised an English friend in early March: "At the present moment the feeling in Montreal and Toronto against the Agreement could hardly be stronger if the United States troops had already invaded our territory."[5]

However uninspiring and uncertain the Conservative opposition at Ottawa had been for some years, the developing anti-reciprocity sentiment in the country soon stiffened its resolve, and infused Robert Borden and his followers with hope that at long last the Laurier regime was vulnerable. Borden had been the Tory chief since 1901, surviving two decisive general election defeats and persistent criticism that he was too gentlemanly and colourless. In addition, there had been the perplexing problem of big business's general orientation towards Laurier, in gratitude for continued tariff protection and railway largesse. Even as the Sifton and the Toronto 18 revolts were unfolding, the latest comic opera coup attempt within the Party very nearly prompted Borden's resignation. One apparent cause had been rumours of moves on his part to form an actual alliance with rebel Liberals like Sifton. In fact, the rumours were true: On March 1 Borden, Sifton, Lloyd Harris, the Liberal M.P. for Brantford, Z. A. Lash of the Toronto 18 and J. S. Willison, the former Liberal who now edited the pro-Conservative Toronto *News*, met with Borden to "proceed at once to organize for the next general election." They won from the Conservative leader a pledge that he would include in his government "reasonable representation . . . of the views of those Liberals who may unite with Conservatives against the policy of reciprocity."[6]

Clifford Sifton as he appeared in 1917.
Public Archives Canada,
PA-28125.

It took time for these new alignments to take root, for the pamphlets to pour off the presses, for the propaganda to reach a public at first genuinely confused and undecided about the merits and demerits of the trade accord. A younger Laurier, sensing the first hint of the marshalling of potent opinion-forming forces against him, probably would have secured dissolution of the House at once, forcing the issue on the electorate while he had the initiative and the advantage of surprise. With every week's delay, however, the Conservatives were emboldened to filibuster the agreement in the Commons. Vain Liberal hopes that the obstruction could be overcome, followed by Laurier's unavoidable absence in London at the Imperial conference and Coronation in the summer, spun the controversy out until late July, when the disgusted and frustrated Prime Minister went off to see the Governor General. The election was set for September 21.

Laurier would tell Lord Grey a few weeks later that "the main issue is strong" and that "we will do much better than I had expected."[7] Certainly most Liberal strength in the Maritimes and the prairie west held well on election day; indeed, in rural Alberta and Saskatchewan there was a landslide for the government, demonstrating the grain growers' gratitude over the proposed reciprocity pact. But the hard assault on the usually solid Liberal Quebec by the *nationaliste*-Conservative forces of Henri Bourassa and Frederick Monk threatened the Prime Minister's political base. Bourassa was not excited by reciprocity — the naval issue remained the bone that he had to pick with Laurier. But opposition was opposition, and it soon became doubtful that Laurier would be able to come out of his home province on election night with his normally unbeatable bloc of Quebec seats.

Accordingly, Ontario became the pivotal province in the election. It had 86 of the 221 Commons seats. Even amid Laurier's great victory of 1908, Ontario had given him only 37 of its seats and 47 per cent of its votes. That strength had been based mainly on the rural Grit Presbyterian-Methodist voting traditions and on the bankrolling assistance of the very kind of big businessmen who in 1911 were deserting the Liberal ship. And in recent years the province's federal Liberal leadership had left a great deal to be desired. Allan Aylesworth, the Minister of Justice, was able and eloquent, but deafness weakened his political effectiveness; and his views on race track betting and the sale of risqué literature were too advanced for the old-line Protestants who were the Party's backbone. William Lyon Mackenzie King, the Minister of Labour, had as yet little political weight across Ontario. In the provincial sphere, the glory days were long gone: in 1905, after 33 years of office, the Party had collapsed amid proven electoral corruption and graft. There were as yet absolutely no signs of revival.[8]

By contrast, the Conservatives were riding high in the province by 1911. An aggressive and popular Premier James P. Whitney led a moderately progressive administration, and had won wide support among the reform minded and many manufacturers with his Ontario Hydro policy of low cost public power. This "businessmen's socialism" was accompanied by initiatives in the industrial and welfare fields which were giving the Conservatives an excellent reputation.[9]

The contrast between this and some aspects of the performance and attitudes of the federal Liberal administration was striking. There had been a number of unseemly graft and corruption scandals involving cabinet ministers and M.P.'s, as well as vast cost overruns and political payoffs connected with construction of the government's National Transcontinental Railway. Public concern was being expressed too at the multiplication of huge corporate trusts and consolidations, without meaningful federal interference. There was also the problem that under Mackenzie King's mild conciliation approach to industrial disputes, working men seeking union recognition frequently were being left unprotected against the wrath of vengeful companies like the Grand Trunk. As the 1910 *Encyclopaedia Britannica* put it, Laurier was "an individualist

Laurier speaking at Moose Jaw: a picture that reflects his times as well as Laurier himself. The beflagged archway behind him, the banner reading "Welcome to our Premier," the incredible hats and dresses

of the little girls, the produce on the platform — all these reflect manners and customs, social and political, that have long since disappeared. *Public Archives Canada, PA-73657.*

rather than a collectivist," who "opposed the extension of the state into the sphere of private enterprise."[10] Ministers who had thought differently — Andrew Blair in 1903 on transcontinental railways, and William Mulock later on government ownership of telephones and telegraphs — had gone their separate ways. Conservative organizers may well have had sound justification early in 1911 for their confidence that, for reasons not connected with reciprocity, all but a handful of Ontario's seats were within their grasp.[11]

Later, when it was all over, Laurier would lament that in Ontario "it was not reciprocity that was turned down, but a Catholic premier." His chief organizer, Alexander Smith, would concede that the anti-Catholic cries had been there, with undoubted effect, but: "You were not defeated by these cries. The cries got the start of you because you had no organization. We had nobody in charge. It was like playing marbles with marbles made out of mud. . . . The two main

causes of your defeat were, first, fifteen years in power and, secondly, no organization." The sensitive Catholic Prime Minister and the frustrated organizer had predictable perspectives, but their analyses showed just how out of touch they had become with the political currents of Ontario. Beyond anti-Catholicism, beyond organization problems, beyond the selfishness of the big interests, beyond even the specifics of the economic issue everyone was debating in the 1911 campaign,

An interesting mixture of transportation modes in Edmonton about 1912: a Grand Trunk Pacific locomotive, an early model "T" Ford car, a covered wagon drawn by oxen, and a street car.
McDermids Studios Ltd.
Public Archives Canada,
C-56695.

W. S. Fielding, c. 1907.
He was Minister of
Finance for the whole of
Laurier's 15 years as
Prime Minister. He was
to hold the same office in
1921-25, in the first
Mackenzie King cabinet.
Canadian Annual Review,
1907. *Metropolitan
Toronto Library Board.*

there was a potent force, a blend of nationalism, anti-Ameri-canism and imperialism, that reflected much of what Canada had become and had experienced in those 15 Laurier years.

The nationalism was not just the class self-interest of the "national" businessmen and their allies in the professions, politics and the press. Clifford Sifton had no reason to exag-gerate to Joseph Flavelle early in the battle when he exlaimed: "since I have been old enough to speak nothing has ever hap-pened in Canada which has created such a spontaneous out-burst."[12] All the years of rhetoric from Laurier and his propagandists about national self-sufficiency and the cultiva-tion of transatlantic rather than continental relationships had been taken seriously. As Senator George Ross, a Liberal and former Premier of Ontario, put it in letters to the Toronto *Globe*, Canada had gone far towards economic maturity on the basis of an east-west transportation system to serve industries protected from U.S. competition, and agriculture thriving on British and European markets for its staples. To alter our economic orientation now, he argued, would be "breaking faith."[13] And W. S. Fielding received early warning from another Ontario Liberal, J. P. Rankin, of the powerful connection which could be made between national and anti-American feeling: "We must steer away from the status of an auxiliary to our big neighbour who professes now to be very friendly to us but in 1898 and previously, when like the Israelites in Egypt, we were making bricks without straw, he would not even give us the straw."[14] Too many Canadians recalled the days of the Americans' unfriendliness and truculence; too many relished the thought of at last thwarting one of their designs.

American champions of reciprocity obligingly helped the Canadian opponents of it. Champ Clark of Missouri, speaker-designate of the House of Representatives, announced that he was for reciprocity "because I hope to see the day when the American flag will float over every square foot of the British-North American possessions clear to the North Pole." Senator McCumber proclaimed: "Canadian annexation is the logical conclusion of reciprocity with Canada." William Randolph Hearst's newspapers were blunt: for example, the New York *American*: "Eventually Canada will come in. That will be when we want her." Privately, President Taft sent former President Roosevelt some very candid predictions of the likely effects of reciprocity:

The amount of Canadian products we would take would produce a current of business between western Canada and the United States that would make Canada only an adjunct of the United States. It would transfer all their important business to Chicago and New York, with their bank credits and everything else, and it would greatly increase the demand of Canada for our manufactures. I see this is an argument against reciprocity made in Canada, and I think it is a good one.

In the 1911 election, for really the first time since 1891, enthusiasts for the Empire connection and defenders of tariff protection for Canadian industry could come together without reservation, using imperialist and nationalist rhetoric and symbolism interchangeably. George Foster in the House of Commons preferred "the old paths, leading east and west, in and out amongst our own people, converging on the great metropolis of the mother land, and which we may follow without uncertainty and without menace to our national existence." Arthur Hawkes, in his popular pamphlet, *An Appeal to the British Born*, said it more forcefully perhaps, describing Canada as economically "in her self-reliant prime," and as "a distinct nationality." "I can conceive of no calling more noble, more full of the dignity of the fruitful years than this calling to create a new nation while we help to re-fashion a venerable and glorious Empire." On September 16, 1911, the Montreal *Star* pulled out all the stops as the electoral battle drew to its close:

> Our vast country will fill up. We will grow from forty to eighty millions. We will be the largest of the British nations. Then the hegemony will come to us; and a Canadian city will be the capital of the British Empire....
>
> We have filled our cities with industries; we have banded our half-continent with railways, we have laughed at leagues of wilderness and leaped over mountains; and we have drawn to our prairies, and the fat fertile land of our older provinces, the sturdiest array of farmers in the world. . . . We have believed in Canada; and she has justified our belief. She is the richest, most promising, most prosperous country in the modern world.

Laurier, his colleagues and his press defenders fought desperately through August and into September to blunt all this emotionalism and to stress the strictly limited scope of the proposed agreement, the continuing determination of the government to keep Canadian industry quite adequately protected and to promote better relations, including reciprocal preferential trade, with Britain. The Prime Minister was still his party's best weapon; the crowds continued to pour out to his meetings, and to cheer and clutch at him as he went by. But the die was cast: power went forever on the night of September 21, 1911. In the gathering gloom of his Quebec City

committee room the old man sat, shocked and stunned, as the returns clacked over the wire: impressive triumphs in Alberta and Saskatchewan; a slim lead in the Maritimes; victory but only just in Quebec; strong Conservative wins in Manitoba and British Columbia; and an unprecedented Tory landslide in Ontario — 73 to 13 with over 56 per cent of the vote going to Borden's candidates. Laurier's majority of 50 in 1908 had become a Conservative one of 47. The Laurier years were over.

Colonel George T. Denison, a leading advocate of Imperial Federation, and for years president of the Canadian branch of the British Empire League, in his Toronto study.
Public Archives Canada, C-70870.

7

The Leader and the Land

Laurier's struggle for power did not end with his defeat in 1911. Within two months he turned 70, and, for a time, the weariness of age and the shock of losing office left him depressed-and despairing. Yet by February 1912, after a by-election victory in Ontario, he promised to remain as leader "so long as you want me and so long as God spares me." Later that year he confided cheerily to a party rally: "At all events I want another tussle with the Tories." Hope and combativeness sprang eternal.

Astonishingly, the Tories very soon appeared vulnerable, their chances for a prolonged ascendency increasingly doubtful. The Conservative-*nationaliste* alliance of 1911 had helped Robert Borden to victory, and had produced cabinet seats for Frederick Monk and two other French-Canadian Conservatives of *nationaliste* leanings. But differences, divisions and disillusionment were not long in coming. Monk resigned from the cabinet in 1912 over Borden's naval policy of an "emergency" gift of 35 million dollars to Britain for dreadnaught construction. And the Prime Minister's failure to safeguard Catholic separate school rights in federal territory ceded to Manitoba, added to the Ontario Conservative government's restrictions on French as a teaching language, further weakened Tory support among French Canadians. Meanwhile, the Liberal dominated Senate blocked the government's naval policy and much of its domestic legislation. For his part, Borden was proving a lacklustre party chief and an uninspiring figure for the public. He was an honest and able man, but utterly devoid of Laurier's flair or his zest for the great game of politics. What was more, an odour of political corruption sur-

rounded the activities of patronage-partial ministers such as
Robert Rogers of Manitoba and Frank Cochrane of Ontario.
The economic slowdown of 1913 was yet another reason to
darken the government's re-election prospects. The Liberal
Party was hardly yet renewed in personnel or policy, but at
least its leader could have some realistic hope by mid-1914 that
an early restoration to office was distinctly possible, perhaps
even likely.

But the outbreak of world war in August of that year,
and the immense scale of Canada's military and economic participation in it over the ensuing four years, revolutionized
Canadian politics, dashing forever Laurier's dreams of vindication and victory. This was not apparent at first, when there
was no more eloquent voice than Laurier's in all of Canada for
a vigorous and unified war effort. He told the House of Commons shortly after the outbreak of hostilities that the struggle
was to "save civilization from the unbridled lust of conquest
and power." But, without illusions, he warned sadly that it
would "stagger the world with its magnitude and horror."

Over the next three years as these features of the war's reality eroded the initial national unity of 1914, it became clear that Canadians really were very diverse in their willingness to regard their involvement in the struggle as overriding all other concerns. As troop commitments soared into the hundreds of thousands, the numbers of recruits available from among the British born, or from British stock — the two groups which had predominated overwhelmingly in the early contingents — dwindled. Most *Québécois*, many farmers, much of the urban working class, and the bulk of the non-Anglo-Saxon immigrants — groups not traditionally touched especially strongly by imperialist and militarist emotions — were not particularly anxious to put their lives on the line. It was principally from among these segments of the population that hesitations and reservations about the full magnitude of the developing Canadian war effort emerged. The Liberal Party had much of its strength based in these groups, yet a good part of its leadership in English Canada was urban, Anglo-Saxon, Protestant and middle class, with very strong cultural and ethnic allegiance to the British and Allied cause. The longer the war was prolonged and the greater the costs in blood, money and social harmony, the more impossible it became to keep the Liberal Party effectively united as a fully functioning force in federal politics. English-French disharmony became clearly the most serious problem.

The Party's unity and sense of common purpose were strained severely in 1916 over an issue not directly related to the war but very much a part of the emerging enmity between French-speaking and English-speaking Canadians to which differences over the war commitment in Europe were so important. The problem, a continuing irritant, was the Ontario bilingual schools dispute. Henri Bourassa's *Le Devoir* denounced the "Boches of Ontario" and Ottawa *Le Droit* decried "Prussianism and barbarity" in that province. The Borden government would not interfere, but Laurier could not afford to be quiet for long, as he dared not allow the *nationalistes* to gain ground once again in Quebec. In 1916, Ernest Lapointe, a Laurier lieutenant, moved that the House of Commons "respectfully suggest" redress of the Franco-Ontarians' grievances. The plea did not budge the authorities at Queen's Park, but it did prompt a rebellion among Liberal M.P.'s from Ontario and the West. Almost all the Ontario men went along grudgingly when Laurier threatened resignation, but all 11 of the Westerners voted against the Lapointe resolution in the House. Laurier was fully aware that lukewarm Quebec support for the war effort and the *nationaliste* tirades, as well as the Anglo-Saxon racism in English Canada which was so stimulated by the war crisis, were mutually reinforcing antagonisms and suspicions. "I have lived too long, I have outlived Liberalism," was his sorrowful reaction as the rents in his Party's fabric showed only too plainly.

The climactic crisis for wartime Canada and Laurier came in 1917. Russia, overwhelmed by revolution, was on her way out of the war, with a vastly strengthened German thrust on the Western Front against the exhausted British and French armies an impending certainty. Germany's resumption of unrestricted submarine warfare, meanwhile, threatened to cut the Allied lifeline from North America. Even the entry in April of the United States on the Allied side could do little, as American mobilization for significant effectiveness on the battlefield necessarily was slow. Sir Robert Borden returned from Britain and the Canadians' battlefront in May 1917 with the conviction that the country's armed strength must not be allowed to fall below the government's most recent commitment of a half-million men. Since the declining voluntary recruitment rate was not even close to keeping up with the soaring casualty figures, Borden, hitherto against conscription, now believed it essential. He invited Laurier to join him in a coalition or union administration on a conscriptionist basis. A general election mandate then would be sought for the new government and its program.

The intricate details of the developments and intrigues concerning conscription and union government belong most properly to the history of Sir Robert Borden's leadership in Canadian affairs. But Laurier was thoroughly caught up in it all and was perhaps the most dramatic figure in the whole tragedy. It was really impossible for him to accept Borden's offer for many and varied reasons. For one thing, his liberalism and anti-militarism, central to his very support of the Allied cause, made him view conscription as improper coercion in the defence of freedom. At the same time, he could not support any measure for war purposes, no matter how sincerely

The famous cartoon of
Laurier by Spy, published
originally in *Vanity Fair*
in London.
Public Archives Canada,
C-1896.

conceived, which threatened to damage French-English unity. He had absolutely no doubt that conscription would have that effect. As he warned the Ontario Liberal Leader, Newton Rowell, any sort of forced enlistment would cause "a line of cleavage in the population . . . for which I will not be responsible." Last, but by no means least, there was politics. Many pro-coalition Tories and Liberals in English Canada believed that Laurier personally could convince a reluctant, annoyed Quebec to go along with conscription, and that he could stand off Bourassa and the *nationalistes* on a conscriptionist win-the-war platform. He knew better, telling Rowell: "Now if I were to waver, hesitate or flinch, I would simply hand over the province of Quebec to the extremists."[1] Besides, it was not unreasonable of him to suppose that from among agrarian, working class and immigrant groups in English Canada he might be able to draw sufficient anti-conscription votes that, with his undoubtedly solid vote in Quebec, he could carry a general election. Everything depended, however, on whether he could keep most of the traditional Liberal leaders in English Canada from bolting the Party.

From June until mid-October of 1917, when a conscriptionist union government finally was formed, Laurier fought a desperate, often brilliant battle. At 75, he still could draw on almost inexhaustible reserves of political sagacity and skill. And the wells of affection and respect for him across the country remained deep. For months, no politically significant federal Liberals of conscriptionist persuasion dared to take their disagreement with their revered "chief" to the point of renouncing his leadership. One factor was that Sir Wilfrid had been a giant among the pygmies of his Parliamentary party for a long time. The courage born of independent habits of thought or a personal power base was largely lacking. Other prominent Liberals, meanwhile — in provincial politics and journalism especially — waited impatiently for the Parliamentarians' leadership. Further blocks to action included the lingering Laurier loyalism of many rank-and-file Liberals in English Canada and an undercurrent of agrarian hesitation, especially in the West, about how conscription would affect the farm labour situation, already heavily strained by productivity demands and the drain of help to the attractively higher pay in war-stimulated industries.

Yet prolonged containment of the conscriptionist and union government pressures which had been building within English-Canadian Liberalism proved impossible. This was especially so among prominent Liberals outside the Parliamentary ranks. Men such as Newton Rowell, the Ontario Liberal chief, and John W. Dafoe, editor of the influential *Manitoba Free Press* of Winnipeg, differed fundamentally from Laurier in their belief that Canada was totally committed as a matured nation to the Allied cause — not merely in aid of Britain but in defence of the survival of Christian and democratic civilization. To them, Laurier's hesitations and half-measures, his concerns about Canada's national unity and his fears about his Quebec power base could not be permitted to stand in the way of a resolute, unrestrained non-partisan maximum Canadian contribution to winning the war. Dafoe and Rowell worked with other prominent Liberals such as J. E. Atkinson of the Toronto *Star*, Stewart Lyon of the Toronto *Globe*, Premier Arthur Sifton of Alberta and J. A. Calder of Saskatchewan to swing substantial Liberal strength, especially in the West, into coalition with the Conservatives. This was aided by two pieces of electoral legislation forced through Parliament by Borden's party. The Military Voters Act enfranchised all service personnel, male or female. If a voter could not identify his constituency, the election officials were empowered to assign his ballot to one. The Wartime Elections Act gave the vote to all female relatives of servicemen and took it away from all immigrants from enemy countries who had come to Canada before 1902. Many conscriptionist Liberals were outraged by the political cynicism reflected in these laws, but a number of them clearly were frightened by the measures into alignment with Borden's forces in a union government. At long last, on October 12, 1917, a coalition was formed under Borden, with Newton Rowell, Arthur Sifton, Calder and six other Liberals joining a farmers' representative and 12 Tories.

"Now I am in the fight to face a murderous winter election even if I have to die for it," Laurier remarked as the new government dissolved Parliament and sought a national mandate. It was his seventh campaign as leader, but he fought with the vigour and intensity of a man half his age and in far better health. His courage and eloquence did not seem one whit diminished. French-speaking Quebec, with Bourassa's forces re-

Sir Wilfrid Laurier with
Sydney Fisher (left) and
Mackenzie King at Quebec
in 1915. In spite of their
long association there are
few pictures of Laurier
and King together.
Public Archives Canada,
C-15567.

inforcing his own, was from the first on his side almost
unanimously. In the Maritimes, although there had been
prominent defections to the Unionist cause, the Liberal organizations largely remained intact, with both conscriptionist
and non-conscriptionist Liberals represented among the Laurier
candidates. In Ontario, the poor 1911 base of Liberal seats,
the defection of the Party's provincial leader and of all but
one of its newspapers, and the hostility of most of the leadership of the prominent Protestant denominations put the Laurier
candidates at a severe disadvantage. In the West, all four provinces were held by Liberal governments, but the Premiers
uniformly were supporting the Unionists; and the normally
pro-Liberal non-Anglo-Saxon immigrant vote had been cut
back severely by the provisions of the Wartime Elections Act.
Yet Laurier was generally received with respect by the mainly
large and attentive audiences which turned out at his meetings.

He promised that as Prime Minister he would vigorously push voluntary recruitment and that he would impose conscription if a majority of Canadians supported it in the referendum he would hold after taking office. That brought or kept a few prominent conscriptionists on board, such as his former cabinet colleague George Graham in Ontario. On the other hand, the considerable anti-conscriptionist feeling among many English-Canadian trade unionists fed Laurier Liberal hopes for a time, as did the widespread agrarian antagonism on the issue, related to the farm labour question. The magnitude of that agrarian discontent could not have been demonstrated more powerfully than by the government's own actions: two weeks before election day it passed an order-in-council exempting persons actively engaged in food production. In spite of a seemingly very successful Laurier tour of the West as the campaign ended, the Unionist strength and appeal solidified.

Throughout, and more than in most elections, there were many atrocious things done and said in the heat of battle, though this was very human. Unionist speakers could not safely address crowds in much of Quebec, but elsewhere propaganda excesses by Unionist publicists balanced the account. The Toronto *News* referred to Laurier as "a demagogue, a charlatan and a mountebank." Dafoe's once proudly Liberal *Free Press* in Winnipeg intoned these lines about the formerly revered Laurier: "Ichabod, O Ichabod. So fallen, so lost, the light withdrawn which once he wore. The glory from his grey hairs gone, forevermore." It must be remembered, however, that when all allowances are made for the cynical motives of participants in that bitter crisis election of 1917, the clash at its roots involved honest and sincere differences on the nature and character of commitment to a titanic war whose outcome was still hanging in the balance and on the survival of a national unity under such severe strain that disintegration of Confederation was by no means impossible. Laurier was one of countless Canadians who were being true to their ideas and ideals, but who in consequence could not expect reasonably to be loved across the land.

Election night, December 17, was a Unionist triumph — 153 seats to 82 and a popular vote of 57 per cent to 39.9 per cent. Quebec went for Laurier by 62 seats to three, with 72.7 per cent of the ballots. In the Maritimes, as usual, the two sides were fairly close, although the Unionists had a clear edge in all provinces except P.E.I. Laurier did pick up ten seats — four each in Nova Scotia and New Brunswick and two in P.E.I. — out of 31 in the region. The Unionist margins elsewhere rivalled or even surpassed Laurier's in Quebec: Ontario, 62.7; Manitoba, 79.7; Saskatchewan, 72.0; Alberta, 61.0; and British Columbia, 68.4.[2] Canada was divided politically on lines frighteningly coincident with French-English differences.

The war was over in 11 months; Sir Wilfrid died of a sudden stroke shortly after on February 17, 1919. When he had breathed his last, the devoted Zoë at his side, the outpouring of national grief and respect was proof that the bitter frustrations, controversies and divisions which had characterized the dusk of his career had not destroyed the essentially positive historical memory most Canadians wished to have of him. It may be that this can be understood best each April in Ottawa when some of the first and loveliest crocuses spring up in colourful profusion at the base of an attractive statue of Laurier; the statue stands on Parliament Hill atop a little ridge beside the East Block cabinet offices, facing towards the Rideau locks and the hotel which bears his name. He stands there, depicted in the breezy optimism and firm strength of the leader in his prime of a nation on the march. In the sunshine, it is easy to understand why for so long he held the affection of his country and the devotion of his followers.

His greatest political achievement, unquestionably, was his forging of Liberal bloc strength in Quebec, making it the basis for his Party's virtual monopoly on federal power in this century. In spite of the *nationaliste* challenge in the last stages of his Prime Ministership, and the electoral inroads of the "unholy alliance" in 1911, he never had less than majority support in Quebec from 1896 onwards. In 1917, with his anti-conscription stand, he took every predominantly francophone constituency in the province, and left his Liberal successors for decades to come in the position of being able to count on almost all of them too. Every Liberal leader since Laurier has eventually become Prime Minister, and most have held that office for an extended period.

While the political effects of Laurier's establishment and consolidation of Liberal power in Quebec are clear, the social implications are much less so. Both federal and provincial

Liberals in Quebec since 1896 usually have been highly conservative in their social and economic policies. Their relationships with the entrepreneurs and financiers in the province –
mostly anglophone – have usually been fairly relaxed and
cozy. Certainly, until at least Maurice Duplessis's time in the
1930s and after, the Liberals had this generally pro-business,
pro-growth orientation, with little if any involvement in, or
reputation for, social reform. The great political revolution of
the 1890s, by which Laurier Liberalism displaced Cartier-
Chapleau Conservatism, was not really a triumph of social reform. In fact, Laurier's party in Quebec eschewed radical
changes in anything. He gained and kept massive support there,
for the most part, for profoundly conservative reasons: reaction against imperialism and the dangers of war and against
ultra-Protestant and anti-francophone bigotry. Since the Conservatives in Quebec usually were fatally compromised on these
very issues by the stands taken by some of their party colleagues elsewhere, the Liberals normally were under no serious
pressure to govern in a very progressive fashion. Only a small
band of Bourassa *nationalistes* – and they fitfully – seriously
challenged Laurier-era Liberalism on grounds of its inadequate
sensitivity to dangerous effects of urbanization and industrialization on Quebec's society and the *survivance* of its cultural distinctiveness. Quebec moved into the post-Laurier years
politically Liberal, but a backward province in terms of the
mass of the population's real sharing in the great wealth flowing
out of her factories and natural resources. The two solitudes
within the province were as separate as ever, except at the top
levels where the Liberal French-speaking politicians and the
English-speaking magnates co-operated comfortably. Sir
Lomer Gouin, with his bushels of company directorships, led
the Quebec phalanx into Mackenzie King's restored Liberal
government at Ottawa in 1921, and was the clearly acknowledged conservative pro-business counterweight to the hard-
pressing western farmer Progressives.

Outside Quebec, Laurier Liberalism did not go so far
in the direction of becoming a business oriented conservative
party. But during the Laurier years there was little the government did which was reformist, whether in improving
political or administrative institutions or with reference to the
special privileges of big interests such as the railways. In 1900,

after Laurier's government had been four years in office, the Toronto *Globe* proposed the establishment of a railway commission to regulate rates, reform of the Senate and the setting up of a civil service commission to oversee "a thoroughly non-partisan service."[3] Laurier exploded to John Willison, the editor, that the program was "of such advanced radicalism that I am at a loss to realize why such a powerful paper as the *Globe* should further it."[4] "As far back as 1897," Willison would recall at the time of Laurier's death, "he [Laurier] said to me 'I wish The Globe would stop urging reforms. Reforms are for Oppositions. It is the business of Governments to stay in office.'"[5] Even the reciprocity policy of 1911 was more a throwback to what had once passed as "Reformism" decades before in an agrarian-commercial society than a perceptive policy for an industrializing country with vastly strengthened national linkages. At the provincial level in English Canada in the decade or so after the turn of the century, it was generally Conservative governments which had a measure of popular success in dealing with the new urban-industrial issues by embracing at least the beginnings of state intervention through improved health, welfare and worker protection measures. In Whitney's Tory Ontario, there was even the phenomenally popular public generation of electrical power — much to the disgust of many champions of private enterprise, including Laurier. "I must tell you frankly," he wrote to a public owner-ship advocate in 1910, "that for my part and with my strong convictions, borrowed from the English Liberal school of politics, I am not much in favour of the growing view of substituting collectivism to individualism in the relations of the government with the people."[6]

Nevertheless, Laurier and the Liberals were no mere care-takers during the 15 busy years of power, making no positive mark on their times and society and leaving no worthwhile heritage behind them. Their incredible political success from the mid-1890s until the beginning of the new century's second decade, was a measure of how well they reflected the aspirations and needs of a society of quick growth and self-confidence. They may have been laissez-faire in a belief that business required little interference or regulation from the federal government, but this did not mean that they were oblivious to business issues, or to how the activities of entrepreneurs could

be aided and stimulated by Ottawa. Their swing towards pro-
tectionism in the 1890s and their lavish assistance to two huge
private transcontinental railways in the next decade made that
plain. When the Canadian Manufacturers' Association met in
convention in Hamilton in 1909 it was estimated in the London
Times that "two-thirds, and certainly a clear majority . . . were
in active sympathy with the Liberal Government in Ottawa."
In addition, the Liberals' policies for western development and

Laurier in old age: one of
the last photographs.
*Public Archives Canada,
C-5851.*

settlement, however flawed in detail, were large in conception, facilitating the quick and generally sound creation of a huge and powerful new partner-region in Confederation. This was done, at least in the early stages, with the active and major participation of the West's own leaders, especially Clifford Sifton.

In fact, Laurier's brilliant early success at incorporating representative, popular and powerful leaders from the various regions made his government for some time perhaps the most impressive array of talent ever to occupy the treasury benches on Parliament Hill. Besides Sifton there were Fielding of Nova Scotia, Blair of New Brunswick, Mowat, Mulock and Cartwright of Ontario, and Tarte of Quebec as men of weight and influence in their own right. As time passed, though new recruits of talent came forward or were promoted, the representativeness and effectiveness of the cabinet and Party leadership diminished, more or less at the same time as the problems of generating growth gradually gave way to dealing with its consequences. Sir Wilfrid's experience and prestige after decades of political prominence, combined with his preference as an aging leader for peace and quiet in surroundings he could control, meant that, by and large, the men he promoted to cabinet rank as the years of power wore on were expected to play largely subservient roles in his administration. As John Dafoe put it: "Men of strong, individual views and ambitions, with reforming temperaments and a desire to force issues, did not find the road to the Privy Council open to them; different qualities held the password."[7] Clifford Sifton was probably the strongest competing personality to sit in cabinet with Laurier, and later recalled how domineering he could be:

> I was not Sir Wilfrid Laurier's colleague for eight years without finding out that he is, despite his courtesy and gracious charm, a masterful man set on having his own way, and equally resolute that his colleagues shall not have their way unless this is quite agreeable to him.

Sifton declined to re-enter the cabinet in 1907 because Laurier refused to permit him to bring with him three or four associates, not dependably obedient to the Prime Minister.[8] At the end, what had been a "ministry of all the talents" was sadly rather second-rate and tired, and not vitally in touch with important currents of public opinion.

But it took a long time for the weaknesses of the men around Laurier to become more significant than the incredible personal magnetism and sensibleness he could bring to bear as leader of his party and government. By the time of his later years in office he had stood in the front ranks politically in the House of Commons and across the nation for more than a quarter-century. He had watched Macdonald manage politicians and public opinion, and had learned much. Like his predecessor, he took care to cultivate backbenchers and journalists and give them the impression that they mattered. "One of the things that endeared him to the younger members of the Party," an M.P. later recalled, "was his habit of meeting us in the corridors, inviting us into his office to smoke a cigarette, and passing five or ten minutes in asking us how Bill Jones was in such and such a village, how so-and-so was and how he was getting along, and inquiring about our own studies and our interests." The M.P. remembered that after a few minutes of this "we returned to the House ready and eager to do anything we possibly could for the leader with whom we were in such perfect communion of heart and mind."[9] The journalist Edward Thomson recorded a corridor encounter in January 1911:

> I met the chief in rotunda of House of Commons. Lord how amiable! Not that he's ever otherwise with me. But this time he came at me through a throng, just to shake hands. And wonder why I had not lately come in for just a pow-pow. "Oh, cos, I knew you must be exceedingly busy." "Well, come to lunch with me on Sunday. Bring the Madame, and we'll have a good talk" — The flowing old charmer! I never could resist his blandishments. Fact is, I love him just as one loves a woman, even though one knows she is a humbug — What matters when she is so delightful?[10]

Even Henri Bourassa, after years of political controversy with Laurier, was able to state: "Although I fought him because of differences of principle, I loved him all my life and he knew that."[11] Laurier could be very tough and resolute in his political relationships, as Joseph Israel Tarte, the Minister of Public Works, found out to his sorrow in 1902 when he tried to promote upward tariff revision and enhance his own political power while the Prime Minister was out of the country and

SUPPLÉMENT   **La Patrie**   ILLUSTR

41e ANNÉE - No 21   MONTRÉAL, SAMEDI, 22 MARS 1919   LE SAMEDI - LE NUMÉRO: DEUX

Les Campagnes Politiques de Laurier

ailing. Sir Wilfrid returned to Ottawa, called for newspaper accounts of Tarte's speeches and then fired the man who had been the mastermind of his victory in Quebec in 1896. Tarte stayed in politics, once more as a Conservative, and for a brief time was something of a thorn in the side of his former chief. Liberal organizers and strategists brewed plans to deal with the renegade, no holds barred. But Laurier had other ideas, as evident in this letter:

> Ottawa, January 16, 1904
>
> My dear Préfontaine,
>
> I am informed that someone in Montreal — I don't know who, but at your orders — is preparing a pamphlet against Tarte, which is a compilation of personal abuse against him.
>
> I write you immediately to warn you against perpetrating, what appears to me to be, a palpable blunder. Abuse does not serve any useful purpose. Its inevitable result is to generate sympathy for the object of the attack.
>
> It must be admitted that, in all justice, Tarte's newspaper is conducted on a most dignified level. He eschews personalities confining himself only to political matters. It is with these same weapons that we must fight him.
>
> Do not allow this brochure to appear. I insist upon this point. If you think I am mistaken, send me the transcript so that I may judge for myself.[12]

Laurier often combined a gentlemanly approach to politics with a shrewd realism. Among his own followers, affection and respect for him were so strong that in the last crisis of 1917 many English-Canadian conscriptionist Liberals ended up supporting him in his campaign against conscription mostly out of personal loyalty.

Canada during the Laurier years was becoming a multicultural society, at least in the prairie west and in the major growing cities. The old familiar British-French character was being altered, although it would not be until years after Laurier's death that this would be reflected powerfully in politics and new forms and styles of nationalism. Laurier and Sifton, for all their loyalty to their own cultural roots, were truly liberal in their readiness to fill up the country with men and women of energy and ambition, of almost any origin. Especially in the years of "good feelings" which followed on Laurier's conciliation of ethnic-sectarian differences in the mid-

OPPOSITE
La Patrie, Montreal, takes an affectionate retrospective look at Laurier's political campaigns in March 1919, a few weeks after his death.
Public Archives Canada, C-15874.

1890s, the optimism of their liberalism made possible a generally open-door approach to immigration just when millions of settlers, from a vast variety of backgrounds, were ready to choose Canada as the place of their dreams. The Canadian community in due course became somewhat divided and unhappy about the social consequences of the coming of some of these "new Canadians." The end of the nation's era of innocence more or less coincided with Laurier's demise, and his successors, of whatever political stripe, had to reflect a more restrictionist public mood.

It was not in immigration matters alone that Canada passed from an atmosphere of optimism to one of anxiety. The Prime Minister at heart was a man of peace, interested essentially in the late nineteenth-century liberal's domestic political concerns. It was only very reluctantly that he was prepared to worry himself about military and security matters: until 1909, he really could not bring himself to take such things very seriously. The Boer War contingents issue had been an aberration in his normal scheme of things, and he had responded to it with a political policy for a temporary crisis. He certainly had not become defence conscious; indeed, his steadfast resistance at subsequent Imperial Conferences against schemes which he feared could draw Canada into the European "vortex of militarism" reflected his own deepest emotions, and not merely a political calculation of Quebec's anti-militarism and isolationism. Only the appearance, beginning in 1909, of insistent and serious pressures within Canada for an active naval defence effort pushed him to action, but his policy of a separate Canadian coastal defence force was really far more an effort at domestic political compromise than an indication that he worried very much about Germany's immediate or near threat to the British Empire's — and hence Canada's — maritime security. It was probably a good thing that when the storm of war came in 1914 it was not Laurier who had to respond to the bugle call and supply stern, aggressive leadership to a non-military people caught up in the most terrible conflagration mankind yet had seen. Still, it should be added that it was Laurier's Minister of Militia until 1911, Sir Frederick Borden, who made substantial improvements in the quality of soldiering and administration in the permanent force and militia, the

essential cadres for the magnificent Canadian Corps of World War I.

In his imperial policy Laurier performed some of his most brilliant work. The force of imperialist enthusiasm among a sizeable number of English Canadians, although vague and varying, was nonetheless a political and national reality in Canada during his Prime Ministership. To ignore or bluntly affront it would have been suicidal, but he confidently believed by the mid-way point of his time in office that he had managed to de-fuse the imperialist issue by stressing Canadian preference for Empire co-operation rather than centralization. While this was not enough for serious hard-line imperialist enthusiasts, it generally satisfied the country for some years, until the naval crisis put a premium on specific action. In spite of Bourassa's criticisms, the bulk of French-Canadian opinion, while hardly pro-imperial, was also content enough with Laurier's vague autonomism until 1909 or 1910. The Drummond-Arthabaska by-election defeat late in 1910 was a clear sign that many *Québécois* were becoming fearful that even Laurier's half-measures in imperial defence pointed Canadians down the road towards foreign war. No national politician in the Canada of these years could have tried harder to bridge the imperialist-*Québécois* gulf, even though without lasting success, as the terrible divisions of the war period would show. His own admiration for British political principles and practices, as well as his love for the classics of English literature, made him something of an intellectual imperialist anyway, and probably helped him to keep lines of communication open to imperialist English Canadians which other French-Canadian politicians would not have been able to set up in the first place. And an English-Canadian Prime Minister during these years of intense challenge for French Canadians' *survivance* would have been very hard pressed indeed to gain and retain their trust.

At least the English-French compromises which he put at the heart of Liberal Party policy and practice did not go out of fashion with the end of his leadership, in spite of the temporary fragmentation of the Party in 1917. However imperfectly, the fact that at least one of the country's major national parties had strong roots in both of the two founding cultures constituted a significant influence for national unity. Of course, *nationalistes*, separatists and near-separatists in Quebec in

Laurier's time and subsequently have never seen his career in that sort of light. Armand Lavergne, one of Bourassa's lieutenants, once described it as "a great illusion" rather than a work of genuine French-English reconciliation and the protection of the French-Canadian minority in Canada.[13] The historian Michel Brunet has listed some of the reasons for that point of view:

> The unsatisfactory compromise Laurier was compelled to accept on the Manitoba school problem; Canada's intervention in the South African War, which fostered and gave vent to the pan-British nationalism of the English-speaking Canadians; Laurier's retreat on the school rights of the Catholic minority when the provinces of Alberta and Saskatchewan were created; the slow progress of bilingualism outside of Quebec; the imperialistic propaganda and the frequent violent outbursts of francophobia and anti-Catholicism of the Anglo-Canadians — reminded the French Canadians that the country in which they lived could not yet be considered as their fatherland.[14]

Yet the English-speaking Canada of Laurier's day was simply too Anglo-Saxon, too North American and too Protestant to make it possible for a French-Canadian Roman Catholic politician to champion even a very mild policy of biculturalism and Catholic minority rights at all forcefully. At least in his long leadership of his Party and the country, he personified the possibilities for fruitful partnership and taught not a few Protestant English Canadians that it was safe, even advantageous, to look to Catholic French Canada for leaders of the highest calibre when the national going got tough.

Laurier's very smoothness, adroitness and flexibility, which so often facilitated compromise and disarmed critics, may also have contributed to or exacerbated his problems, perhaps even helped to bring about his downfall. His "sunny ways" sometimes attracted support from odd combinations of people, many of whom would end up severely disillusioned. For example, the Anglo-Saxonist imperialist zealot George Denison and the *nationaliste* Henri Bourassa were both very much in his corner in the early years of power, but eventually deserted him. John Dafoe and John Willison were his devoted journalistic admirers for years, but came to distrust his willingness to compromise on issues like separate schools and defence, where

OVERLEAF
The funeral cortège passing the Chateau Laurier. He was buried in Notre Dame Cemetery, where a striking monument marks his grave. *Public Archives Canada, PA-24972.*

they believed certain principles ought to govern. On this last score, Canon Lionel Groulx, after dining with Laurier one evening during the war, mused:

> The impression that he left with me that day, an impression that I retained and later confirmed in my studies of minority schools, was that of a great, honest man in his basic character, but a politician given to organizing his views and his method of thinking according to party interests and philosophy. I had the impression of a liberal whose disappointments and the recent abandonments by some of the most eminent of his supporters had not broken his confidence in men, but I felt too that he was a party leader more intelligent than courageous, more flexible than unyielding, that his optimism, perhaps unconsciously the rules of the Parliamentary political game and, most of all, his habit of aiming always at power inclined him to a faith without limits in what he called "sunny ways," that is to say compromises if not compromising as a system, to the point that no right, however sacred, could justify a political crisis or a racial conflict.[15]

John Willison, perhaps too bitter to be fair, remarked at the time of Laurier's death: "Sir Wilfrid was unmoral, not deliberately immoral. After forty-five years of age he had no sentiment nor any strong conviction on any subject."[16] Augustus Bridle, in his charming *The Masques of Ottawa*, written in 1921, had this to say of Laurier:

> A writer who at various periods of time was very intimate with Laurier thinks he was a man of deep emotions. This may be doubted. A man who talked so easily and was so exquisitely conscious of himself could scarcely be considered spiritually profound. Other men and events played upon him like the wind on an Aeolian harp. He was tremendously impressionable; and by turns grandly impressive. . . .
>
> There never was a moment of his waking life when he could not have been lifted into a play. His movements, his words, his accent, his clothes, his facial lineaments were never commonplace, even when his motives often may have been. He was Debussy's Afternoon of a Faun; poetry and charm all the days of his life.[17]

Bridle should have added that the poetry and charm were not just for effect, as Mackenzie King observed for his diary one January night in 1910, minutes after seeing Laurier in his private office on Parliament Hill:

He looked very tired & frail, after the long night's sitting, but so splendid in his dignified appearance to his fingertips he is artistic, & he shews his feelings in the delicate way he moves his fingers & poised them as tho' holding a flower between the thumb & forefinger when seeking to make a point. His head, side face, as he rests in his seat is like an eagle's.[18]

Groulx, Willison and Bridle were doubtless correct in their assessments that Laurier was no idealistic crusader, at least after the days of his youth. But he was not several decades at the centre of the nation's life without leaving a deep and positive imprint. It may be that he learned so well the lessons of Canadian statecraft in the later nineteenth century that he really could not respond adequately to the problems of the twentieth. Had he been less brilliant, less a master of politics, he would not have survived to be outdated. At the heights his higher qualities were given without stint to his country when strong leadership was needed to raise Canadians' sights at a time of vast change and great opportunity.

Notes

Chapter 1

1. J. W. Dafoe, *Laurier: A Study in Canadian Politics* (Toronto: McClelland and Stewart, 1964), p. 24.
2. J. S. Willison, *Reminiscences, Political and Personal* (Toronto: McClelland and Stewart, 1919), p. 166.
3. Dafoe, p. 26.
4. *Ibid.*, p. 31.
5. Toronto *Globe*, August 24, 1889.
6. M. Pope, ed., *Public Servant: The Memoirs of Sir Joseph Pope* (Toronto: Oxford, 1960), p. 104.
7. Laurier Papers, Mulock to Laurier, December 9, 1893.
8. *Ibid.*, Laurier to Oscar McDonnell, July 14, 1893. McDonnell was editor of Ottawa *Le Canada*.
9. Willison Papers, Laurier to Willison, December 31, 1895.
10. Willison, *Reminiscences*, p. 270.

Chapter 2

1. P.A.C., Minto Papers, Minto to Arthur Elliot, February 26, 1899 and May 5, 1901.
2. P.A.C., Rodolphe Lemieux Papers, Laurier to Lemieux, December 1, 1892 (author's translation).
3. London *Times*, June 14, 1897, pp. 4, 5.
4. Toronto *Evening News*, October 11, 1899.
5. Laurier Papers, Laurier to L. Gabriel, January 6, 1900.
6. W. S. Evans, *The Canadian Contingents and Canadian Imperialism* (Toronto: Publishers' Syndicate, 1901), pp. 24, 25.
7. Toronto *Mail and Empire*, November 3, 1900.
8. Toronto *World*, November 5, 1900.
9. Toronto *News*, November 6, 1900.
10. *Debates*, March 13, 1903, p. 75; *Le Devoir*, June 27, 1911.
11. P.A.C., G. T. Denison Papers, Denison to Chamberlain, April 18, 1903.
12. Toronto *News*, May 26, 1903.
13. Manitoba *Free Press*, October 22, 1903.
14. Laurier Papers, Laurier to Sifton, October 8, 1903.

Chapter 3

1. J. A. Hobson, *Canada Today* (London: T. Fisher Unwin, 1906), p. 3.
2. These and the earlier immigration figures have been drawn from *Census of Canada*, 1911, Vol. 2, pp. 440-443; *Census of the Prairie Provinces*, 1936, Vol. 1, pp. 32, 434, 898; and Statistics Canada, *Canada One Hundred, 1867-1967* (1967), p. 99.
3. Particularly good on the West's urban growth surge are Paul Voisey, "The Urbanization of the Canadian Prairies, 1871-1916," *Social History*, VIII (No. 15, May 1975), p. 84; and J. M. S. Careless, "Aspects of Urban Life in the West, 1870-1914," in A. W. Rasporich and H. C. Klassen, eds., *Prairie Perspectives 2* (Toronto: Holt, Rinehart & Winston, 1973), p. 29.
4. See T. W. Acheson, "The National Policy and the Industrialization of the Maritimes, 1880-1910," *Acadiensis* (Spring, 1972), pp. 3-28.
5. Stephen Scheinberg, "Invitation to Empire: Tariffs and American Economic Expansion in Canada," in G. Porter and R. Cuff, eds., *Enterprise and National Development: Essays in Canadian Business and Economic History* (Toronto: Hakkert, 1973), p. 86; H. V. Nelles, *The Politics of Development* (Toronto: Macmillan, 1974), pp. 228, 229, 348.
6. Cited, R. Graham, *Arthur Meighen*, I *The Door of Opportunity* (Toronto: Clarke, Irwin, 1960), p. 309.
7. Douglas Library, Queen's University, J. W. Flavelle Papers, Flavelle to Willison, April 3, 1903.
8. Rupert Brooke, *Letters from America* (London: Sidgwick and Jackson, 1947), p. 50.
9. See J. Russell Harper, *Painting in Canada: A History* (Toronto: University of Toronto Press, 1966), and D. W. Buchanan, ed., *Canadian Painters: From Paul Kane to the Group of Seven* (Oxford: Phaidon, 1945), for further detail.

Chapter 4

1. On this see Terry Copp, *The Anatomy of Poverty: The Condition of the Working Class in Montreal, 1897-1929* (Toronto: McClelland and Stewart, 1974).
2. Cited, J. S. Woodsworth, *My Neighbour* (1911; reprinted, University of Toronto Press, 1972), pp. 136-138.

3. See the excellent book by Alan F. J. Artibise, *Winnipeg: A Social History of Urban Growth, 1874-1914* (Montreal: McGill-Queen's University Press, 1975).

4. Copp, *op. cit.*, pp. 34, 44, 50, 140-143.

5. Public Archives of Canada, W. L. M. King Papers, Diary, cited R. M. Dawson, *William Lyon Mackenzie King*, I *1874-1923* (Toronto: University of Toronto Press, 1958), p. 67.

6. On this and other aspects of federal labour policy in these years the best available source is J. A. Atherton, *The Department of Labour and Industrial Relations, 1900-1911* (M.A., Carleton University, 1972).

7. Cited, Dawson, *King*, I, p. 142.

8. Laurier Papers, King to Laurier, August 4, 1910.

9. The story of the "navvies" is found most conveniently in Donald Avery, "Canadian Immigration Policy and the 'Foreign' Navvy, 1896-1914," CHA, *Historical Papers, 1972*, pp. 135-136.

10. This is traced in W. D. Atkinson, *Organized Labour and the Laurier Administration: The Fortunes of a Pressure Group* (M.A., Carleton University, 1957).

11. The pages which follow, on the prairie reactions, are based on material in the excellent thesis by Marilyn J. Barber, *The Assimilation of Immigrants in the Canadian Prairie Provinces, 1896-1918: Canadian Perception and Canadian Policies* (Ph.D., University of London, 1975), with the permission of the author.

Chapter 5

1. Lionel Groulx, *Mes Mémoires*, I *1878-1915* (Montreal: Fides, 1970), pp. 104, 105 (author's translation).

2. Laurier Papers, Laurier to J.-B.-A. Casgrain, April 20, 1905.

3. André Siegfried, *The Race Question in Canada* (Toronto: McClelland and Stewart, 1966), p. 185.

4. Laurier Papers, Laurier to L. Brousseau, August 24, 1907.

5. P.A.C., Lord Grey Papers, Grey to J. Bryce, June 2, 1909.

6. P.A.C., Borden Papers, J. D. Reid to Borden May 25, 1911.

7. Grey Papers, Grey to Lord Crewe, December 16, 1910.

8. Cited, Mason Wade, *The French Canadians*, I (Toronto: Macmillan, 1968), p. 578.

9. *Ibid.*, pp. 581, 582.

10. Laurier Papers, Laurier to R. Lemieux, August 6, 10, 11, 19, 1910; Lemieux to Laurier, December 26, 28, 1910.

Chapter 6

1. H. Moorehouse, *Deep Furrows* (Toronto and Winnipeg: G. J. McLeod, 1918), p. 72.
2. Quoted, J. W. Dafoe, *Laurier*, p. 84.
3. *Canadian Annual Review*, 1911, pp. 48, 49.
4. Halifax *Herald*, March 8, 1911.
5. Grey Papers, Grey to Sir William Harcourt, March 6, 1911.
6. Willison Papers, Vol. 105, Memorandum, undated.
7. Lord Grey Papers, Laurier to Grey, August 23, 1911.
8. See Paul D. Stevens, "Laurier, Aylesworth and the Decline of the Liberal Party in Ontario," Canadian Historical Association, *Historical Papers*, 1968, pp. 94-113.
9. Charles W. Humphries, "The Sources of Ontario Progressive Conservatism," C.H.A., *Historical Papers, 1967*, pp. 118-129.
10. *Encyclopaedia Britannica*, Eleventh Edition (Cambridge: Cambridge University Press, 1910), p. 287.
11. R. Cuff. "The Conservative Party Machine and the Election of 1911 in Ontario," *Ontario History*, LVII (September, 1965), pp. 149-156.
12. Flavelle Papers, Sifton to Flavelle, March 2, 1911.
13. Toronto *Globe*, September 27, 30 and November 4, 1910.
14. W. L. M. King Papers, Rankin to Fielding, November 1, 1910 (copy).

Chapter 7

1. P.A.C., N. W. Rowell Papers, Laurier to Rowell, June 2, 1917.
2. J. M. Beck, *Pendulum of Power: Canada's Federal Elections* (Toronto: Prentice-Hall, 1968), p. 148.
3. Toronto *Globe*, January 9, 1900.
4. Willison Papers, Laurier to Willison, January 10, 1900.
5. *Ibid.*, Willison to Col. Hugh Clark, March 12, 1919.
6. Laurier Papers, Laurier to D. R. Wood, December 24, 1910.
7. Dafoe, *Laurier* (1963), p. 84.
8. Willison Papers, Sifton to Willison, August 27, 1907.

9. N. Ward, ed., *A Party Politician: The Memoirs of Chubby Power* (Toronto: Macmillan, 1966), p. 73.

10. A. S. Bourinot, ed., *Edward William Thomson (1849-1924): A Bibliography with Notes and Some Letters* (Toronto: private, 1955), p. 24.

11. Ottawa *Citizen*, January 23, 1935.

12. Laurier to R. Préfontaine, January 16, 1904, in possession of Mr. Matthew Teitelbaum of Ottawa.

13. A. Lavergne, *Trente ans de vie nationale* (Montreal: Editions du Zodiaque, 1934), p. 70 (author's translation).

14. M. Brunet, "The French Canadians' Search for a Fatherland," in P. Russell, ed., *Nationalism in Canada* (Toronto: McGraw-Hill, 1966), pp. 53, 54.

15. Lionel Groulx, *Mes Memoires*, I *1878-1915* (Montreal: Fides, 1970), p. 324 (author's translation).

16. Willison Papers, Willison to Col. Hugh Clark, March 12, 1919.

17. "Domino," *The Masques of Ottawa* (Toronto: Macmillan, 1921), p. 41.

18. P.A.C., King Diary, January 31, 1910.

Bibliography

SIR WILFRID LAURIER has generally been given very generous treatment by contemporaries and scholars alike. Of the biographies, three stand out. Sir John Willison's *Sir Wilfrid Laurier and the Liberal Party* (2 vols., Toronto: G. N. Morang, 1903) was the first serious full-scale attempt. While overly admiring, it contains many useful insights and is especially good on Liberal struggles with the Church in Quebec during Laurier's early career. O. D. Skelton's *Life and Letters of Sir Wilfrid Laurier*, originally published 1921 (Toronto, McClelland and Stewart Carleton Library edition, 1965) was the first account to be based on the Laurier correspondence collection, and covers a great deal of ground. Both Skelton and Joseph Schull, *Laurier: The First Canadian* (Toronto: Macmillan, 1965) have seen their subject as so heroic and admirable, however, that thorough examination of any of his failures or deficiencies and fair treatment of his opponents are largely lacking.

A couple of smaller, semi-biographical volumes are excellent. John W. Dafoe, the Winnipeg journalist and a friend of Laurier who became a resolute opponent, wrote the sparkling analytical essay *Laurier: A Study in Canadian Politics*, originally published 1922 (Toronto, McClelland and Stewart, Carleton Library edition, 1964), which should not be missed. And H. Blair Neatby's *Laurier and a Liberal Quebec* (Toronto: McClelland and Stewart, Carleton Library edition, 1973) is the best study available of Laurier's background in and relations with his home province.

Works in French have tended to be rather sketchy. However, L. O. David's *Laurier: sa vie, ses oeuvres* (Beauceville: L'Eclaireur, 1919) is perhaps the most distinguished. Robert Rumilly wrote *Sir Wilfrid Laurier: Canadien* (Paris: Librairie Ernest Flammarion, 1931), but had more of value to say in his biographies of Mercier, Mgr. Laflèche and Henri Bourassa, and in the first 23 volumes of his *Histoire de la province de Québec* (Montréal: Editions Bernard Valiquette, n.d.). On Laurier speeches, there is the excellent three volume compilation by A. D. DeCelles, *Discours de Sir Wilfrid Laurier* (Montréal, Beauchemin, 1909-1920).

Two articles deserve mention. Mason Wade's "Sir Wilfrid Laurier" in C. T. Bissell, ed., *Our Living Tradition: First Series* (Toronto: University of Toronto Press, 1957), pp. 89-104, is an interesting re-statement of the familiar theme about Laurier the hero of French-English harmony. Paul Stevens in "Wilfrid Laurier: Politician," pp. 69-85 of Marcel Hamelin, ed., *The Political Ideas of the Prime Ministers of Canada* (Ottawa: University of Ottawa Press, 1969) offers evidence on Laurier's Machiavellian and other talents in day-to-day politics.

Excellent general background on the Laurier years is available in two volumes in the Canadian Centenary Series, published by McClelland and Stewart of Toronto. Peter B. Waite's *Arduous Destiny: Canada, 1874-1896* (Toronto: McClelland and Stewart, 1971) and Ramsay Cook and R. Craig Brown's *A Nation Transformed: Canada, 1896-1921* (Toronto: McClelland and Stewart, 1974) contain a good deal on Laurier himself, plus a mine of bibliographical and footnote information.

Since the appearance of the Waite and the Cook and Brown volumes, three important books on themes and personalities of the Laurier years have appeared. Paul E. Crunican's, *Priests and Politicians: Manitoba Schools and the Election of 1896* (Toronto: University of Toronto Press, 1974) is a fascinating peek into the political attitudes and actions of the Quebec hierarchy at a critical time. And R. Craig Brown's *Robert Laird Borden, A Biography, Vol. I: 1854-1914* (Toronto: Macmillan, 1975) provides a distinguished first installment on a full biographical study of Laurier's chief federal political opponent. On a broader scale, the recent volume in this series by John English, *Borden: His Life and World* (Toronto: McGraw-Hill Ryerson, 1977) is valuable.

Index